Contents

Acknowledgments

The Central Office of Information would like to thank the Foreign and Commonwealth Office and the Ministry of Defence for their co-operation in compiling this book.

Photograph Credits

Numbers refer to the pages of the illustration section (1–4): Nigel Huxtable front cover, p.1 (top and bottom), p.2 (top and bottom), p.3 (top); Andy Mason p.3 (bottom); *Soldier* magazine p.4 (top); Liz Raymond-Cox p.4 (bottom).

Britain and the
Gulf Crisis

London: H M S O

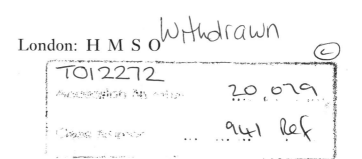

Researched and written by Reference Services, Central Office of Information.

© Crown copyright 1993
Applications for reproduction should be made to HMSO.
First published 1993

ISBN 0 11 701734 5

Introduction

The Gulf crisis was initiated by Iraq's invasion of its small neighbour, Kuwait, on 2 August 1990. The ruling Al-Sabah royal family was deposed and Iraq sought to maintain a military occupation of Kuwait, as an annexed territory, in defiance of a series of United Nations Security Council resolutions.

Iraq's invasion provoked not only condemnation but also unprecedented co-operation in the international community to reverse the aggression. A multinational military force—Britain's contribution to which was the largest of any European country—was assembled in the Gulf region during the months after August 1990.

When it became clear that Iraq would respond neither to the UN Security Council resolutions nor to other diplomatic initiatives, armed force was initiated by the international coalition in mid-January 1991. Following a brief and successful campaign, the coalition forced an Iraqi withdrawal from Kuwait and hostilities were suspended at the end of February.

The following chapters describe Britain's role:

—in the diplomatic efforts to reverse Iraq's aggression and in the multinational military deployment and offensive in the Gulf; and

—in post-war operations to protect Kurdish civilian refugees from the Iraqi regime and in the maintenance of allied pressure on Iraq to honour the terms of the Gulf peace settlement.

The book covers events up to Autumn 1992. Information on subsequent developments may be found in *Current Affairs – A Monthly Survey,* published by HMSO.

Detailed information on the experiences of the British Forces in the Gulf campaign is contained in *The Shield and the Sabre: the Desert Rats in the Gulf,* by Nigel Pearce, published by HMSO.

Background to the Iraqi Invasion

The Al-Sabah family has ruled Kuwait since the early eighteenth century, long before the creation of Iraq in 1921. The territory later came under Turkish suzerainty. In 1899 Kuwait became a British protectorate and in 1913 Britain and the Turkish Ottoman Empire signed a convention recognising Kuwait's autonomy. The convention was not ratified because of the onset of the first world war (1914–18).

In 1914 Britain recognised Kuwait as an independent state under British protection. After the end of the first world war Turkey renounced all rights and titles to subordinate territories in its former empire.

Kuwait's borders with the new kingdom of Iraq were drawn in 1923 and were accepted by Iraq in 1932 when it became an independent state.

British protection ceased in 1961 when Kuwait became a fully independent state. Shortly after, Iraq laid claim to the whole of Kuwait. Fearing an Iraqi invasion, Kuwait requested assistance from Britain which sent troops in 1961. These were later withdrawn and replaced by troops from member countries of the Arab League. These in turn were withdrawn in 1963 when Iraq formally recognised Kuwait's sovereignty and independence.

In July 1990 Iraq and Kuwait became involved in a dispute over oil pricing and production levels and over Iraqi debts to Kuwait. Iraq's main demand was that Kuwait and the United Arab Emirates should cut oil production in order to maintain prices. Iraq also stated that it should not have to repay the loans of many

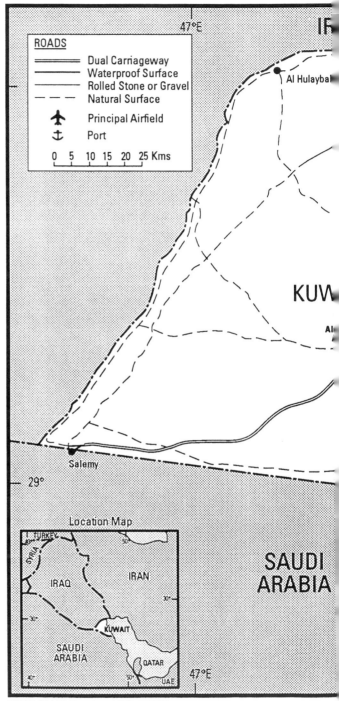

ROADS

Dual Carriageway
Waterproof Surface
Rolled Stone or Gravel
Natural Surface

✈ Principal Airfield
⚓ Port

0 5 10 15 20 25 Kms

47°E

IR

Al Hulayba

KUW

Al

Salemy

29°

Location Map

TURKEY
SYRIA
IRAQ
IRAN
KUWAIT
SAUDI
ARABIA
QATAR
UAE

47°E

SAUDI
ARABIA

11888 (CAD) October 1992 772/92

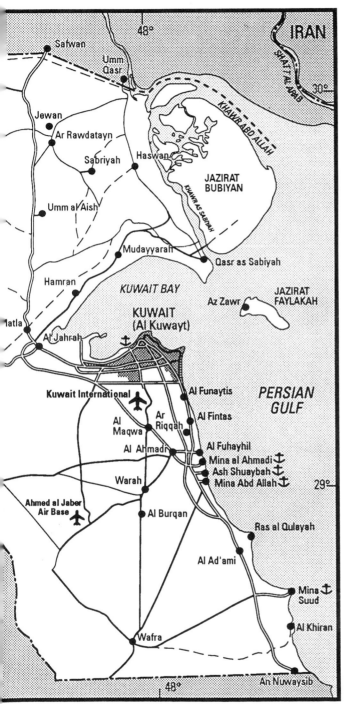

billions of dollars received from Kuwait during the Iran–Iraq war (1980–88). As the dispute developed, Iraq deployed troops near the border with Kuwait.

Diplomatic efforts were made by members of the Arab League to defuse the situation. Iraq and Kuwait agreed to bilateral talks in Jedda on 1 August and Iraq assured Egypt and Saudi Arabia that it had no intention of invading Kuwait. Despite these assurances, President Saddam Hussein of Iraq ordered his forces to invade Kuwait on 2 August. He did so under the pretext of responding to a request from a revolutionary government which, he alleged, had overthrown the Al-Sabah family. This revolutionary government was in fact non-existent. The whole of Kuwait was occupied by the invading Iraqi forces and Iraq announced its annexation of the country on 8 August.

International Reaction

The British Government's unreserved condemnation of Iraq's action was a view shared widely within the international community. This was quickly reflected in the UN Security Council with the adoption of resolution 660 (1990) on 2 August 1990. The mandatory resolution (approved, in the absence of Yemen, by 14 votes to 0) demanded the immediate and unconditional withdrawal of Iraqi forces and called for a negotiated settlement between Iraq and Kuwait.

On 3 August 1990 the United States and the then Soviet Union issued a joint statement condemning the 'illegal invasion' and demanding the restoration of the sovereignty, national independence and territorial integrity of Kuwait. The statement appealed for a halt to all arms deliveries to Iraq and concluded: 'Governments which resort to flagrant aggression must know that the international community cannot and will not reconcile itself to aggression or assist in it.' This view was reaffirmed by the then US President, George Bush, and the then Soviet President, Mikhail Gorbachev, at a summit meeting in Helsinki, Finland, on 9 September.

Imposition of Sanctions

On 4 August Britain and its European Community partners imposed an embargo on oil imports from Iraq and Kuwait, and Iraqi assets in the territory of Community member states were frozen. (The British Government had frozen Kuwaiti assets in

Britain immediately after the invasion at the request of the Kuwaiti ambassador to prevent their transfer to Iraq or to any Iraqi-installed regime.) A Community embargo was also placed on sales of arms and other military equipment to Iraq, and any military co-operation was suspended. Technical and scientific co-operation, together with trade concessions to Iraq, were similarly suspended.

Because of Iraq's failure to comply with resolution 660, the UN Security Council imposed comprehensive mandatory economic sanctions against Iraq on 6 August. Resolution 661 (1990), approved by 13 votes to 0 (with Yemen and Cuba abstaining), prohibited all imports originating in Kuwait or Iraq (predominantly oil). It also banned the export of any commodities and products to either country, including armaments and military equipment but excluding medical supplies and, in humanitarian circumstances, foodstuffs.

The resolution also required states to deny funds or any other financial or economic resources to the Iraqi Government or to any commercial, industrial or public utility undertaking in Iraq or Kuwait. The assets of the legitimate government of Kuwait and its agencies were to be protected and no regime set up by the Iraqi occupying forces was to be recognised. A sanctions committee was established by the Security Council to monitor compliance with provisions of the resolution.

The then British Permanent Representative to the United Nations, Sir Crispin Tickell, said that the Security Council had a particular responsibility for small and vulnerable states and that practical action was required against Iraq. The Council needed to set a new precedent for the better management of a world order based on respect for law, sovereignty and territorial integrity.

Annexation of Kuwait

Meeting again on 9 August, the Security Council condemned the Iraqi annexation of Kuwait announced the previous day. Resolution 662 (1990) described the annexation as 'null and void' and called upon all states and international organisations 'not to recognise that annexation and to refrain from any action or dealing that might be interpreted as an indirect recognition of that annexation'.

Arab Reactions

The majority of Arab countries opposed Iraq's aggression against Kuwait and some contributed troops to the multinational defence force (see p. 20). Member states of the Gulf Co-operation Council[1] condemned Iraq's occupation as a breach of both international and Islamic law.

At an emergency summit meeting of the Arab League held in Egypt on 10 August, the majority of the 20 countries attending, including Egypt, Syria and Morocco, backed a resolution to send a pan-Arab force to defend Saudi Arabia and other Gulf states against attack. They also voted in favour of imposing economic sanctions against Iraq. Algeria and Yemen abstained while Jordan, Mauritania and Sudan entered reservations. The resolution was rejected by Libya, Iraq and the Palestine Liberation Organisation (PLO). Tunisia did not attend.

Britain rejected any linkage between the Arab–Israeli and Gulf conflicts as suggested in the Iraqi President's proposal, first put forward on 12 August, of parallel talks on Iraq's occupation of

[1]Comprising Bahrain, Kuwait, Oman, Qatar, Saudi Arabia and the United Arab Emirates.

Kuwait, Israel's occupation of Palestinian land and the Syrian presence in Lebanon. Britain made it clear that there could be no reward for aggression by Iraq and that no compromise solution would be acceptable.

Foreign Nationals

Although referred to as 'guests' by the Iraqi Government, many foreign nationals particularly from Western countries were barred from leaving Iraq and Kuwait until an Iraqi announcement of unconditional release on 6 December. During that period they were considered hostages under Iraqi control. In addition to deportation from Iraqi-occupied Kuwait to Iraq, some were placed at strategic sites as a human shield against possible attack by the forces ranged against Iraq.

UN Security Council resolution 664 (1990), unanimously adopted on 18 August, demanded that Iraq permit and facilitate the immediate departure of the nationals of third countries, and grant immediate and continuing access of consular officials to them. The resolution also called for the rescinding of Iraq's order, announced on 9 August, that diplomatic missions in Kuwait had to close and transfer their activities to the Iraqi capital of Baghdad by 24 August. Britain kept its embassy open, in defiance of the Iraqi order, to protect British nationals in Kuwait.

Iraq continued to detain foreign nationals as hostages until December, although women and children and some of the sick and elderly had earlier been allowed to leave. In a move rejected by Western leaders as cynical manipulation, President Saddam Hussein announced on 18 November that Iraq would release foreign hostages in batches over three months starting on Christmas Day. However, on 6 December the Iraqi President then announced that all foreign nationals held in Iraq and Kuwait would be unconditionally released.

In response, the Foreign and Commonwealth Secretary, Douglas Hurd, emphasised that pressure would be maintained on Iraq. On 6 December he said: 'Three main requirements were laid down . . . by the Security Council of the United Nations—the unconditional withdrawal of Iraqi forces from Kuwait, the restoration of the Kuwaiti Government and the freeing of all hostages. If the third of the requirements is carried through, that is welcome news, but it does not detract in the least from the importance of the others.'

Enforcement of Sanctions

On 25 August the Security Council approved resolution 665 (1990) by 13 votes to 0 (Yemen and Cuba abstaining), aimed at ensuring stricter compliance with the economic sanctions against Iraq. It called upon those member states deploying maritime forces to the Gulf area, in support of the legitimate Government of Kuwait, to 'halt all inward and outward maritime shipping in order to inspect and verify their cargoes and destinations and to ensure strict implementation of the provisions related to such shipping laid down in resolution 661 (1990)'. Full UN authority was therefore given to the enforcement of sanctions by naval force if necessary.

On 13 September the Security Council adopted resolution 666 (1990), by 13 votes to 2 (Yemen and Cuba voting against), requesting that the UN Secretary-General monitor, on a continuing basis, the availability of food in Iraq and Kuwait. If there arose an urgent humanitarian need to supply foodstuffs, these would be provided and distributed through the UN in co-operation with the appropriate agencies.

Diplomatic Premises in Kuwait

Incursions by Iraqi forces into the diplomatic premises in Kuwait of certain European Community and other states provoked Security Council condemnation in resolution 667 (1990), unanimously adopted on 16 September. It demanded that Iraq comply with its obligations under international law (the Vienna Convention) by ensuring the safety and wellbeing of diplomatic and consular personnel and premises in Kuwait and in Iraq and by taking no action to hinder the diplomatic missions in the performance of their functions.

In response to Iraq's violations of diplomatic privilege, Britain and its European Community partners agreed on 17 September to expel all Iraqi military attachés and to restrict the movement of remaining embassy staff. Britain also issued deportation orders against some Iraqi nationals for reasons of national security. Iraq took retaliatory measures against diplomatic representatives from Western countries in Baghdad.

EC–Soviet Statement

On 28 September European Community member states and the then Soviet Union adopted a joint statement on the Gulf crisis saying that Iraq's action had violated fundamental principles of the UN Charter and international law and could not be tolerated.

They expressed satisfaction at the high degree of consensus within the UN Security Council and the international community as a whole concerning the need to restore international legality. The preservation of this consensus and full compliance with the sanctions agreed upon by the Security Council were necessary to achieve a political solution to the crisis.

Air Embargo

On 25 September an air embargo was instituted against Iraq and Kuwait by resolution 670 (1990) which was adopted by the UN Security Council by 14 votes to 1 (Cuba voting against). It confirmed that the imposition of sanctions applied to all means of transport including aircraft. It also required states to detain or deny port entry to Iraqi-registered shipping involved in the violation of sanctions.

Addressing this meeting of the Security Council, Mr Hurd welcomed the resolve of the international community to resist Iraqi aggression, which had faced the 'post-cold war world with its first crucial test'. Iraq's action was 'a breach of international law, given greater horror by the pillage of Kuwait, the ruthless treatment of foreign hostages, [and] Kuwaitis alike', and could not become a pattern for international relations in the future.

Mr Hurd recognised that there were many small countries with reason to fear the attentions of a more powerful neighbour. If Iraq was allowed to retain the spoils of conquest, other would-be aggressors would take heart.

Maintenance of Pressure on Iraq

In a parliamentary statement on 24 October, Mr Hurd stated that pressure on Iraq in the form of diplomatic isolation, the economic blockade and the threat of forcible expulsion from Kuwait would be maintained. Noting evidence of brutality, murder and destruction by Iraqi forces in Kuwait, he declared that Iraqis at all levels of military or civilian authority had to be reminded that they were 'personally responsible under the Geneva Convention for illegal acts committed as occupiers in Kuwait'.

European Community heads of Government, meeting in Rome on 27 and 28 October, denounced Iraq's persistent violation of international law and demanded the immediate and unconditional withdrawal of Iraqi forces from Kuwait. The destructive occupation of Kuwait, the oppression and deportation of its population, the holding of foreign hostages and the violation of diplomatic conventions could not be tolerated.

UN Security Council resolution 674 (1990), approved on 29 October by 13 votes to 0 (Yemen and Cuba abstaining), condemned Iraqi hostage-taking and the mistreatment of foreign nationals and Kuwaitis. States were invited to supply the Council with information regarding substantiated cases of human rights violations by Iraq against their nationals.

The Security Council also pointed out that Iraq was liable for any loss, damage or injury caused to foreign nationals and corporations as a result of its invasion and occupation of Kuwait. States were invited to collect information regarding such claims, with a view to establishing arrangements for restitution or financial compensation.

Authorisation of the Use of Force

On 29 November, the Security Council approved resolution 678 (1990), the effect of which was to authorise the use of military force against Iraq if its forces had not been withdrawn from Kuwait by mid-January 1991.

The resolution, which was opposed by Yemen and Cuba with the People's Republic of China abstaining, offered Iraq one final opportunity, 'as a pause of goodwill', to comply with the demands of the Security Council. If Iraq had not done so by 15 January, the resolution authorised UN member states co-operating with the

Government of Kuwait to 'use all necessary means to uphold and implement resolution 660 and all subsequent relevant resolutions and to restore international peace and security in the area'.

Addressing the Security Council on 29 November, Mr Hurd said that the obliteration of one UN member state by another threatened the whole structure of international order. He continued: 'It is important to be clear that after this resolution [678] there is an option for peace and the Iraqis hold it in their hands. It is for them to use that option or to discard it. The international community has not added today to its demands. It is not asking anything except the reversal of the aggression—namely full compliance with previous resolutions.'

The Security Council could not be accused of impatience with Iraq. By mid-January, at the end of this further period of grace, the aggression against Kuwait would be nearly six months old. Mr Hurd added: 'The military option is reality, not bluff. If it has to be used it will be used with the full backing of the Council.' Britain's support for military action in the last resort to force an Iraqi withdrawal from Kuwait was affirmed by the House of Commons on 11 December.

While on a visit to the United States on 21 December, the Prime Minister, John Major, maintained that it was in the interests of the international community to ensure that the Iraqi President gained nothing from the way he had behaved. He continued: 'The message of the Security Council resolutions is entirely clear. We have no intention of attacking him before 15 January. After 15 January we expect him, or before if he will, to move back to within his own territory of Iraq. . . . If he stays within Kuwait then it is perfectly clear that we may have to expel him forcibly.'

On 3 and 13 January 1991, the British Government ordered the expulsion of most Iraqi embassy staff and made deportation orders against Iraqi citizens whose presence in Britain was deemed a threat to national security. British diplomats were withdrawn from Baghdad.

Amnesty International Report

On 19 December 1990 Amnesty International released a comprehensive report on human rights violations in Kuwait since the Iraqi invasion. The report, based on medical evidence and on interviews with victims and eyewitnesses, was submitted to all members of the UN Security Council and to the Iraqi Government. Hundreds of people, it stated, had been tortured and killed, and many thousands imprisoned under the Iraqi occupation.

Most of the abuses detailed in the report took place in the first three months after the invasion, when dissent among Kuwaitis and other nationals was widespread and its suppression ruthless. Such abuses perpetrated by Iraqi forces in Kuwait 'have been the norm for people in Iraq for more than a decade'.

In a statement issued on 19 December 1990, the British Government said that returning British nationals had confirmed accounts of Iraqi brutality in Kuwait.

Peace Efforts

On 30 November 1990 the US President offered direct talks with Iraq to bring about a peaceful solution. The purpose of the offer was not to negotiate with Iraq but to leave the Iraqi leadership in no doubt as to the determination of the international community to see its withdrawal from Kuwait.

The then US Secretary of State, James Baker, and the then Iraqi Foreign Minister, Tariq Aziz, met in Geneva, Switzerland, on 9 January. Despite more than six hours of talks the meeting concluded in disagreement. Mr Baker regretted the absence of 'any Iraqi flexibility whatsoever'. He added that if the occupation of Kuwait continued, Iraq would be choosing a military confrontation that it could not win and which would have devastating consequences.

Mr Aziz affirmed the Iraqi contention that withdrawal from Kuwait should be linked to the resolution of the Palestinian question. He claimed that Iraq was prepared for hostilities, adding that Iraq would attack Israel if it was itself attacked.

All subsequent diplomatic efforts in pursuit of a peaceful solution were unsuccessful. Iraq refused to meet with representatives of the European Community, and a visit to Baghdad by the UN Secretary-General on 12 and 13 January in an attempt at mediation with Iraq proved fruitless. Rejecting these peace efforts, President Saddam Hussein described the crisis as 'no longer an issue about a governate and a part of Iraq; it has become a symbol of the whole nation, and a symbol of a confrontation and an area of honour'.

A final appeal for peace was issued on 15 January by the UN Secretary-General after Security Council discussions failed to reach agreement on a new peace initiative.

Allied Military Deployment

A multinational military force was assembled in the Gulf region from August 1990 at the request of Kuwait, Saudi Arabia and other Gulf states in response to the military threat from Iraq and in support of UN Security Council resolutions. About 40 nations contributed, the United States providing the largest military contingent. Britain and France, among the European contributors, also deployed substantial forces in the region. Arab contingents came from the countries of the Gulf Co-operation Council and from Syria, Egypt and Morocco. (See table on p. 20 for a full list of contributors to the coalition effort.)

Each country deployed forces at the invitation of the Gulf states to assist them in the exercise of their right of individual and collective self-defence under Article 51 of the UN Charter.[2]

United States Action

The US President announced on 7 August 1990 that US troops, warships and aircraft would be sent to Saudi Arabia, at the request of King Fahd, to deter the threat from Iraq. In a further statement

[2]Article 51 says: 'Nothing in the present Charter shall impair the inherent right of individual or collective self-defence if an armed attack occurs against a Member of the United Nations, until the Security Council has taken measures necessary to maintain international peace and security. Measures taken by Members in the exercise of this right of self-defence shall be immediately reported to the Security Council and shall not in any way affect the authority and responsibility of the Security Council under the present Charter to take at any time such action as it deems necessary in order to maintain or restore international peace and security.'

Table 1 Contributions to the Coalition Effort in the Gulf

	Took part in offensive air ops in Iraq & Kuwait	Took part in offensive land ops in Iraq & Kuwait	Took part in offensive naval ops in the Gulf	Took part in naval embargo ops	Took part in mine-clearance ops ①	Defended key areas in Saudi Arabia ②	Deployed Medical Units ③	Provided practical or financial assistance to the coalition ④	Took part in defensive ops in the NATO area
Afghanistan (Mujahideen)						●			
Argentina				●					
Australia			●	●			●		
Bahrain	●	●						●	
Bangladesh						●	●		
Belgium				●	●		●	●	●
Canada	●		●	●	●		●	●	
Czechoslovakia							●		
Denmark				●			●	●	
Egypt		●			●				
France	●	●		●	●	●	●	●	
Germany					●		●	●	●
Greece				●					●
Hong Kong								●	
Hungary							●		
Italy	●		●	●			●	●	
Japan					●			●	
South Korea							●	●	
Kuwait	●	●	●	●				●	
Luxembourg								●	
Morocco						●			
Netherlands			●	●	●		●	●	●
New Zealand							●	●	
Niger						●			
Norway				●			●	●	●
Oman		●							
Pakistan					●	●	●		
Poland							●		
Portugal								●	●
Qatar	●	●						●	
Romania							●		
Saudi Arabia	●	●	●	●		●		●	
Senegal						●			
Sierra Leone							●		
Singapore							●		
Spain				●				●	●
Sweden							●		
Syria		●							
Turkey								●	●
UAE	●	●							
UK	●	●	●	●	●	●	●	●	●
US	●	●	●	●	●	●	●	●	●

Note:

① Covers both land mines in Kuwait and sea mines in the Gulf. Includes operations after 28 Febuary.

② Includes those nations who deployed forces to Saudi Arabia but did not take part in offensive operations.

③ Includes chemical decontamination units.

④ Does not include provision of bases in the Gulf region. Other nations may also have provided assistance on a bilateral basis.

Source: *Statement on the Defence Estimates: Britain's Defence in the 90s, Vol 1, 1991.* Cm 1559–I. HMSO, 1991.

on 8 August, he denounced Iraq's aggression and defined four principles guiding US policy. These were the:

—immediate and unconditional withdrawal of Iraqi forces from Kuwait;

—restoration of Kuwait's legitimate Government;

—maintenance of security and stability in the Gulf; and

—protection of US citizens abroad.

Recognising Iraq's willingness to use force to advance its ambitions and given the presence of its enormous war machine on Saudi Arabia's border, the United States had responded to the Saudi call for military assistance.

By the beginning of November, the United States had deployed about 230,000 troops in the Gulf region, accompanied by formidable naval and air power. On 8 November President Bush announced that this substantial military presence would be further reinforced by additional aircraft carriers, air force units, tanks and extra troops. By the beginning of 1991 US forces were thought to number over 400,000, providing an effective offensive capability against Iraq.

British Measures

On 8 August the British Government announced that it would contribute forces 'to a multinational effort for the collective defence of the territory of Saudi Arabia and other threatened states in the area and in support of the United Nations embargo'. The statement added: 'We are in urgent touch with the United States, our other allies and our friends in the Gulf on the contribution which we can best make in response to a request [for assistance].' Commenting on the Government's decision, Mr Hurd said that the request for

British assistance had come from King Fahd. The subsequent British deployment was known as Operation GRANBY.

By the beginning of October 1990 British forces committed to the Gulf operation numbered over 15,000. Naval deployment comprised two frigates, two destroyers, three mine-countermeasures vessels and attendant support ships. Air power comprised three squadrons of Tornado and Jaguar aircraft, accompanied by Rapier surface-to-air missiles and backed up by tanker and air transport support, as well as Nimrod maritime patrol aircraft. Land forces mainly comprised the 7th Armoured Brigade, including 120 tanks.

On 22 November the Defence Secretary, Tom King, announced that British ground forces would be increased to divisional strength with the deployment of the 4th Brigade, together with an additional artillery brigade, a divisional headquarters and supporting arms. The deployment of further missile batteries and helicopters as well as two more mine countermeasures vessels was announced at the same time. Certain key skills required for this deployment were met by the selective use of reservists.

Air power was reinforced by the deployment of a further 18 Tornado aircraft in the first half of January 1991. In all, some 45,000 British personnel were committed to Operation GRANBY.

Iraqi Capability

Prior to the Gulf war, through a sustained military build-up under President Saddam Hussein, Iraq possessed conventional armed forces comprising about 1 million men, 5,500 tanks, 3,500 pieces of artillery and 800 combat aircraft.

In addition, Iraq was believed to aspire to nuclear-weapon and biological warfare capabilities and had stocks of chemical weapons which it employed on several occasions during the war with Iran between 1980 and 1988 and also against Kurdish civilians in the north of the country.

Iraqi troops deployed in Kuwait and southern Iraq were estimated to number about 590,000 by mid-January 1991.

Operation Desert Storm

British, US and other coalition air forces began attacks on military installations and other associated strategic targets in Iraq and Kuwait on 16–17 January 1991 at about midnight Greenwich Mean Time. This action, authorised by resolution 678, was taken after extensive consultation between the main coalition governments and only when no other effective course remained. The whole campaign, involving naval operations and a brief ground offensive, was successfully concluded 43 days later.

The coalition's aims remained those set out in the UN Security Council resolutions:

—to secure a complete and unconditional Iraqi withdrawal from Kuwait;

—to restore the legitimate Government of Kuwait; and

—to re-establish international peace and security in the area.

In a statement on 17 January 1991, the Prime Minister said that only with the greatest reluctance and as a last resort did he accept the use of force against Iraq, but President Saddam Hussein's intransigence had left no other option.

Britain believed that if Iraq were to gain from its aggression against Kuwait, other small countries with larger and potentially hostile neighbours would be likely to face similar dangers. It also believed that the failure to secure Iraq's withdrawal would have grave implications for the balance of power throughout the Middle East. With the acquisition of more devastating weapons and an unchecked appetite for conquest, Iraq would pose a greater danger in the future.

The international community had no quarrel with the people of Iraq. Mr Major explained that coalition attacks were being directed at Iraq's military capability and that coalition pilots had been instructed to avoid causing civilian casualties or damaging sites of religious and cultural significance so far as was possible. Support for British forces participating in the military campaign was confirmed in a debate in the House of Commons on 21 January.

In a declaration on 17 January, member states of the European Community expressed their regret that the use of force had become necessary. They reiterated their support for the objectives contained in the Security Council resolutions and expressed solidarity with the international coalition's forces in the Gulf.

President Bush announced that military action was being taken in accordance with UN resolutions and with the consent of the US Congress, and he stressed that the goal of the operation was not the conquest of Iraq but the liberation of Kuwait.

The Air Campaign

At the start of the air campaign the coalition forces had over 2,400 combat and support aircraft. The military objectives were to:

—disrupt Iraq's command, control and communications;

—destroy Iraq's nuclear, biological and chemical warfare capability;

—establish air superiority;

—sever the supply routes supporting the occupation of Kuwait; and

—attack the Iraqi forces in the Kuwait Theatre of Operations (KTO).

Air forces from ten coalition countries took part in the campaign (see table on p. 20). Command and control arrangements were agreed to enable these forces to work together effectively. All coalition aircraft operated in accordance with a common plan drawn up in the multinational headquarters in Riyadh, Saudi Arabia. About 110,000 operational sorties of all kinds were flown during the campaign.

British Tornado ground-attack aircraft were in the forefront of operations to establish air superiority, destroying Iraqi airfield installations and radars. This prevented Iraqi aircraft from getting airborne in significant numbers and made it difficult for the Iraqis to detect where attacks were being launched. Tornado air defence aircraft contributed to continuous-combat air defence patrols throughout the campaign.

As coalition aircraft destroyed Iraqi hardened aircraft shelters, around 120 of the most modern Iraqi warplanes took refuge in Iran.[3] Thirty-five Iraqi aircraft were shot down and an unknown number were destroyed in shelters or otherwise on the ground.

Ground-attack Tornados also concentrated on the disruption of the supply routes supporting Iraqi forces in Kuwait, freeing more US aircraft to carry out attacks against Iraqi forces, particularly tanks and artillery equipment, in the KTO. The deployment of some Tornado and Buccaneer aircraft in a laser-designator role increased the ability to carry out precision bombing attacks. British Jaguar aircraft concentrated their ground attacks on Iraqi positions

[3]The Iranian Government observed a policy of neutrality during hostilities and impounded the Iraqi aircraft.

to the south of Kuwait City and flew some sorties against Iraqi naval targets.

During hostilities the Royal Air Force carried out over 4,000 combat, and 2,500 support missions, dropping over 3,000 tonnes of weapons. Six Tornados were lost on missions over Iraq.

Prisoners of War

In a breach of the Geneva Conventions, Iraq failed to provide the International Committee of the Red Cross (ICRC) with any information about the prisoners of war of coalition forces which it held. Seven airmen were shown on Iraqi television, including two British officers.

Only when, under the ceasefire terms (see p. 33), Iraq released the prisoners and the bodies of coalition personnel that it was holding, was it discovered that seven of the 12 missing British officers were still alive.

Naval Operations

The aircraft and cruise missiles of US ships in the Gulf were an integral part of the air campaign. The coalition also deployed amphibious forces to threaten a landing on the coast of Kuwait, thereby forcing the Iraqis to keep large numbers of troops in positions defending the beaches, where they played no part in the main land battle (see below).

The coalition aim was to gain control of the northern Gulf, neutralising the threat to coalition vessels and vital port facilities in Saudi Arabia from Iraqi missile attack. Britain deployed up to 26 ships in the area during the conflict and, just before the suspension of hostilities came into effect (see p. 31), the nine coalition vessels in the most forward positions in the Gulf were all British.

The Royal Navy's mine countermeasures vessels played the major role in clearing a path through the extensive Iraqi off-shore minefields. This enabled amphibious forces to threaten the Kuwait coast and US battleships to carry out shore bombardment. Royal Navy ships also took part in co-ordinated patrols in the eastern Gulf.

Iraqi Operations

The suppression of operations by Iraq's Scud missile delivery systems, both fixed sites and mobile launchers, was of particular importance to the coalition during the campaign in the light of attacks on Israel and Saudi Arabia. In all, Iraq fired 86 Scuds before the suspension of hostilities: 40 against Israel, 44 against Saudi Arabia and two in the direction of Bahrain and Qatar. The missiles were fired indiscriminately against civilian population centres as terror weapons, but many were countered by the US-developed Patriot anti-missile system. Operations by coalition air and special forces also did much to reduce Iraq's capability to launch these weapons.

On 21 January Mr Major condemned the Iraqi missile attacks, recognising that it was Saddam Hussein's aim 'to draw Israel fully into the war in the hope of inflaming Arab opinion, breaking the multinational coalition and inciting a holy war'. At the same time he stressed that the international community would need to renew its efforts to solve the Arab–Israel problem once the Gulf conflict was over.

Israel was not a part of the coalition and, despite its right of self-defence, took no part in the operations against Iraq.

Iraqi offensive ground operations were limited to some unsuccessful probing attacks across the border between Kuwait and

Saudi Arabia at the end of January. These attacks were repulsed by Saudi, Qatari and US forces.

Environmental Damage by Iraq

Soon after the start of the coalition air campaign, Iraq began to release large quantities of oil into the Gulf by opening the pipeline to an offshore terminal as well as emptying five laden oil tankers. The spillage was stopped on 26 January when US aircraft carried out a precision attack against machinery regulating the flow of oil.

On about 22 February it became apparent that Iraq was systematically destroying oil facilities and public and private buildings in Kuwait, and setting fire to Kuwait's oil wells. Large numbers of Kuwaitis were also being detained and taken to Iraq.

Diplomatic Moves Preceding the Ground Offensive

On 15 February the Iraqi Government declared its 'readiness to deal with Security Council [resolution] 660 of 1990 with the aim of reaching an honourable and acceptable political solution including withdrawal [from Kuwait]'. However, a series of conditions was attached to this offer which found no favour at the United Nations and was rejected by Britain, the United States and the Arab partners in the coalition.

Between 18 and 22 February the Soviet Government put forward two sets of peace proposals in talks with the then Iraqi Foreign Minister, Mr Aziz. The British and United States Governments welcomed the Soviet attempts to find a solution but considered that the Soviet proposals fell short of the UN Security Council requirements and were therefore unacceptable.

In a final effort to obtain Iraqi compliance, the coalition governments issued a statement on 22 February setting out clear conditions which Iraq needed to meet to bring about a cessation of hostilities. It set out a timetable for the withdrawal of Iraq's forces from Kuwait, the release of prisoners of war and detainees, the removal of explosive devices, and the cessation of flights by combat aircraft and of destructive acts against Kuwait and its people.

The statement made it clear that if Iraq informed the United Nations of its acceptance before 17.00 Greenwich Mean Time on 23 February, the coalition would not launch a ground offensive. Iraq, however, defied the ultimatum.

Ground Campaign

The coalition ground forces had been deployed to the south of Kuwait, opposite the Iraqi forces and in the optimum position to defend against an attack on Saudi Arabia. Since Iraq was deprived of the use of reconnaissance aircraft following the start of the air campaign, the coalition was able to redeploy forces to the west, without detection, in order to outflank the Iraqi positions.

The ground assault, involving combat forces from 11 countries, was launched in the early hours of 24 February, by which time it was estimated that perhaps 40 per cent of Iraqi tanks and artillery in the KTO had been destroyed by allied air raids and shelling. Naval gunfire and amphibious feints diverted Iraqi attention to the coast, while coalition frontal assaults were launched through the defensive fortifications in southern Kuwait. At the same time coalition forces, including the British 1st Armoured Division, advanced from the west.

The offensive achieved all military objectives within four days and with only light casualties on the coalition side. On 27 February Mr Major confirmed that Kuwait City had been liberated and that British troops had repossessed the British Embassy there.

Suspension of Offensive Operations

Early on 28 February, after consultation with coalition partners, the US President announced the decision to suspend offensive combat operations in the Gulf with effect from 05.00 Greenwich Mean Time. He declared that the coalition's military objectives had been achieved and that Kuwait was once more in the hands of Kuwaitis.

Shortly afterwards, Iraq announced its observance of the ceasefire and notified the UN Secretary-General of its agreement to 'comply fully with resolution 660 and all other Security Council resolutions'.

In a parliamentary statement on 28 February, Mr Major explained that the coalition decision to suspend operations had been taken as soon as it became clear that Kuwait had been liberated and that Iraq's army had been defeated. Economic sanctions against Iraq would remain in force until the UN Security Council decided to lift them. Mr Major added that Britain would seek a commitment from Iraq to destroy, under international supervision, all its ballistic missiles and weapons of mass destruction, and not to acquire such weapons in the future.

The Prime Minister recognised that a durable peace had to provide for the security of Kuwait and other countries in the Gulf and had to deal with other regional problems, principally the Palestinian question. He stressed that the coalition had no quarrel with the Iraqi people, who were themselves the victims of the war to which the Iraqi leadership had condemned them.

In the course of the conflict, it was estimated that 42 Iraqi divisions, 3,300 Iraqi tanks, 2,200 artillery pieces and 2,200 armoured personnel carriers had been destroyed, captured or disabled.

Contributions to Britain's Costs

The total additional defence costs of Operation GRANBY were of the order of £2,500 million, which would be spread over several years. Cash contributions from other countries to Britain to offset these costs totalled about £2,000 million.

This figure comprised about £660 million from Kuwait; £580 million from Saudi Arabia; £275 million each from Germany and the United Arab Emirates; £183 million from Japan; £16 million from South Korea; £15 million each from Belgium and Hong Kong; and £8 million from Denmark.

Assistance in kind—such as transport and logistic items, ammunition, medical services, fuel, food and accommodation—was also received from 18 countries.

The Ceasefire

UN Security Council Resolution 686

On 2 March 1991 the UN Security Council set out the terms for a permanent ceasefire in the Gulf in resolution 686 (1991) which was approved by 11 votes to 1 (Cuba) with 3 abstentions (Yemen, the People's Republic of China and India).

Affirming that all 12 previous UN resolutions on the Gulf crisis continued to have full force and effect, resolution 686 required that Iraq:

—rescind immediately its actions purporting to annex Kuwait;

—accept in principle its liability under international law for any loss, damage or injury arising in regard to Kuwait and third states, and their nationals and corporations, as a result of the invasion and illegal occupation of Kuwait;

—immediately release, under the auspices of the International Committee of the Red Cross or Red Crescent societies, all Kuwaiti and third country nationals detained by Iraq, and return the remains of any deceased Kuwaiti and third country nationals so detained; and

—immediately begin to return all seized Kuwaiti property.

The resolution further required that Iraq:

—cease hostile or provocative actions by its forces against all member states, including missile attacks and flights of combat aircraft;

—designate military commanders to meet with coalition counter-parts in order to arrange for the military aspects of an early cessation of hostilities;

—arrange for the immediate release of all prisoners of war, under the auspices of the International Committee of the Red Cross, and return the remains of any deceased personnel of the coalition forces; and

—assist in identifying Iraqi mines, booby traps and explosives as well as any chemical and biological weapons and material in Kuwait, in those areas of Iraq under temporary coalition occupation and in the adjacent waters.

During the period required for Iraq to comply with the above demands, the provisions of Security Council resolution 678 (1990) (see p. 14) would remain valid. The decision of the international coalition to commence immediately the release of Iraqi prisoners of war, as required by the terms of the Third Geneva Convention of 1949, was welcomed.

Resolution 686 also requested that the United Nations, its member states, specialised agencies and other associated international organisations take all appropriate action to assist in the reconstruction of Kuwait.

On 3 March the Iraqi Government announced that it had 'taken note of the text of Security Council resolution 686 of 1991' and would 'meet its obligations in accordance with the said resolution'. On 5 March the Iraqi Revolution Command Council announced that all of its decisions regarding Kuwait since 2 August 1990 (the date of the Iraqi invasion) were rescinded.

On 4 and 5 March Iraq handed over a total of 45 allied prisoners of war to the International Committee of the Red Cross.

UN Security Council Resolution 687

Terms for a formal settlement of the Gulf war were set out in UN
Security Council resolution 687 (1991) on 3 April 1991. It was
approved by 12 votes to 1 (Cuba) with 2 abstentions (Yemen and
Ecuador), and was formally accepted by Iraq.

It affirmed all 13 previous resolutions on the Gulf crisis,
'except as expressly changed below to achieve the goals of this resolution, including a formal ceasefire'.

Borders

The resolution required Iraq and Kuwait to respect the international boundary and the allocation of islands set out in the agreement
made by both countries in October 1963. The UN Secretary-
General would assist in the demarcation of the boundary and the
Security Council would guarantee its inviolability (see p. 53).

Peacekeeping

A UN observer unit would be established to monitor a demilitarised zone extending 10 km (about 6 miles) into Iraq and 5 km
(about 3 miles) into Kuwait from the international boundary agreed
in 1963. Violations of the zone or potential threats to peace would
be immediately reported to the Security Council.

The resolution noted that the deployment of the observer unit
would enable member states co-operating with Kuwait to bring
their military presence in Iraq to an end.

Weapons of Mass Destruction

Chemical, Biological and Missile Capabilities
The resolution invited Iraq to reaffirm unconditionally its
obligations under the 1925 Geneva Protocol prohibiting the use of

chemical and biological methods of warfare and to ratify the 1972 convention against biological weapons.

It went on to require Iraq to accept unconditionally 'the destruction, removal, or rendering harmless', under international supervision, of:

—all chemical and biological weapons and related development and production facilities; and

—all ballistic missiles with a range greater than 150 km (93 miles) and related maintenance and production facilities.

For the implementation of the Security Council decision, Iraq was required to submit a declaration on the locations, amounts and types of these weapons to the Secretary-General within 15 days of the adoption of the resolution. Within 45 days of the passage of the resolution, the Secretary-General would submit a plan for the approval of the Security Council providing for:

—the formation of a Special Commission to carry out immediate on-site inspection of Iraq's biological, chemical and missile capabilities (based on Iraq's declaration and the designation of any additional locations by the Special Commission itself);

—the yielding by Iraq of its biological and chemical weapons and facilities to the Special Commission for destruction or neutralisation; and

—the destruction by Iraq, under supervision of the Special Commission, of all its long-range missile capabilities including launchers.

These requirements were to be completed within 45 days of the Security Council's approval of the plan. Iraq was also required to 'unconditionally undertake not to use, develop, construct or acquire' chemical and biological weapons or ballistic missiles. The resolution requested that the Secretary-General, in consultation with the Special Commission, develop a plan for the monitoring and verification of Iraq's compliance.

Nuclear Capability

Regarding Iraq's nuclear capacity, the resolution invited Iraq to reaffirm unconditionally its obligations under the Treaty on the Non-Proliferation of Nuclear Weapons.[4]

The resolution required that Iraq undertake:

—not to acquire or develop nuclear weapons or 'nuclear-weapons-usable material' or related research and development facilities;

—to submit a declaration on the locations, amounts and types of such weapons and facilities in Iraq to the Secretary-General and the International Atomic Energy Agency (IAEA)[5] within 15 days of the adoption of the resolution; and

—to place 'all of its nuclear-weapons-usable materials under the exclusive control, for custody and removal, of the IAEA'.

Iraq was required to accept a schedule under which the IAEA, with the assistance of the Special Commission (see above), would:

[4]Signed in 1968, the Non-Proliferation Treaty has about 140 countries party to it, including Iraq. It bans the transfer of nuclear weapons or other nuclear explosive devices to non-nuclear-weapon states by nuclear-weapon states and their acquisition or manufacture by non-nuclear-weapon states. Non-nuclear-weapon states which are party to the treaty have to conclude safeguards agreements with the IAEA in order to prevent diversion of nuclear energy from peaceful uses to nuclear weapons or other nuclear explosive devices.

[5]The IAEA's aim is to prevent the diversion of nuclear energy from peaceful uses to nuclear weapons or other nuclear explosive devices through safeguards arrangements negotiated with individual states. In addition, it verifies the obligations of states which are signatories of the Non-Proliferation Treaty.

—carry out immediate on-site inspection of Iraq's nuclear capabilities (based on Iraq's declaration and the designation of any additional locations by the Special Commission);

—develop a plan for submission to the Security Council within 45 days providing for the destruction or neutralisation of all Iraq's nuclear capabilities;

—carry out the plan within 45 days following approval by the Security Council; and

—develop a further plan, taking into account the rights and obligations of Iraq under the Non-Proliferation Treaty, for the monitoring and verification of Iraq's compliance with its undertakings. This would include an inventory of all nuclear materials in Iraq 'to confirm that IAEA safeguards cover all relevant nuclear activities in Iraq'.

The military limitations imposed upon Iraq by the resolution represented 'steps towards the goal of establishing in the Middle East a zone free from weapons of mass destruction and all missiles for their delivery and the objective of a global ban on chemical weapons'.

Compensation

The resolution reaffirmed Iraq's liability under international law 'for any direct loss, damage, including environmental damage and the depletion of natural resources, or injury to foreign governments, nationals and corporations, as a result of Iraq's unlawful invasion and occupation of Kuwait'. It also demanded that Iraq honour its foreign debts.

The Security Council decided to create a fund to pay compensation for claims against Iraq (see p. 53). The fund would be administered by a commission and would be financed by a percentage of

Iraq's oil revenues. Within 30 days of the adoption of the resolution, the Secretary-General would present recommendations to the Security Council for:

—administering the fund;

—determining the level of Iraq's contributions, taking into account the needs of its people, its economic capacity and its foreign debts;

—ensuring that payments are made by Iraq to the fund;

—arranging the allocation of funds and the payment of claims; and

—evaluating losses, listing claims and verifying their validity and resolving disputed claims.

Sanctions

On sanctions against Iraq, the resolution declared that with immediate effect Iraq could import foodstuffs and 'materials and supplies for essential civilian needs'. Every 60 days the Security Council would review restrictions on the sale or supply of non-military goods to Iraq.

The embargo on Iraqi exports would be removed once the Security Council had approved the mechanism for compensation and Iraq's weapons of mass destruction had been eliminated.

The ban on the sale or supply to Iraq of arms, military technology and support services, including conventional equipment, would be maintained indefinitely. The Secretary-General would draw up guidelines to facilitate full international implementation of the embargo. The Security Council would review the ban relating to conventional arms on a regular basis, 'taking into account Iraq's compliance with this resolution and general progress towards the control of armaments in the region'.

Other Provisions
The resolution declared that Iraq should facilitate the repatriation of all Kuwaiti and third country nationals by extending all necessary co-operation to the International Committee of the Red Cross.

Iraq was required to condemn and renounce international terrorism.

Upon Iraq's formal acceptance of the provisions of the resolution, 'a formal ceasefire is effective between Iraq and Kuwait and the member states co-operating with Kuwait in accordance with resolution 678 (1990)'.

British View
Speaking after the adoption of the resolution the British Permanent Representative, Sir David Hannay, told the Security Council on 3 April that the expulsion of Iraq from Kuwait had marked a 'clear, firm and effective determination of the world community not to allow the law of the jungle to overcome the rule of law'.

He continued: 'Just as the Security Council had the primary responsibility to reverse the aggression, so it has also to lay sound foundations for the future and to ensure that we are not again confronted with such a ruthless and comprehensive challenge to international law'.

Sir David said that the boundary between Iraq and Kuwait had been settled in 1963 but the border had not been demarcated and Iraq had raised territorial claims which were incompatible with the 1963 agreement. Britain considered that the rapid demarcation of the border, monitored by a UN observer unit and guaranteed by the Security Council, would prevent a repetition of Iraqi aggression.

Sir David considered that Iraq's weapons of mass destruction should be eliminated because 'Iraq alone in the region has not only developed many of these appalling weapons, it has actually used them against both a neighbouring state and against its own population: and it has made the threat of their use part of the daily discourse of its diplomacy'. He added that action against Iraq's weapons of mass destruction should be part of a wider arms-control strategy for the whole Middle East region. The conventional arms embargo against Iraq had to be strictly maintained.

Iraq had to pay compensation, Sir David said, for the destruction of Kuwait's economy, infrastructure and natural resources and for the environmental damage to the whole Gulf region. However, the Security Council recognised that the Iraqi economy should not be crippled by the burden of payment. The resolution therefore made financial provision for meeting claims out of a limited proportion of Iraq's future oil revenues.

Iraq's economy had been adversely affected by the high level of military expenditure under President Saddam Hussein's regime (28 per cent of Iraq's gross national product in 1988). Without the burden of such expenditure Iraq, with its oil wealth, could assure both 'a reasonable measure' of economic development and prosperity and meet claims for compensation.

Deployment of UN Peace Force

On 9 April 1991 the Security Council unanimously adopted resolution 689 (1991), providing for the deployment of the United Nations Iraq–Kuwait Observer Mission (UNIKOM) in the demilitarised zone and comprising up to 1,440 armed and unarmed military personnel provided by UN member states. UNIKOM assumed responsibility for the demilitarised zone on 6 May, allowing the last coalition forces to leave southern Iraq.

Iraqi Refugees

After the provisional Gulf war ceasefire, an armed rebellion against President Saddam Hussein's regime broke out, particularly in the south of Iraq and among the Kurdish population in the north. Despite initial rebel success, troops loyal to the regime violently suppressed the revolt during March 1991.

Some two million Iraqi Kurdish refugees converged on the border areas with Iran and Turkey seeking sanctuary from reprisals by the Iraqi army. The plight of the refugees, lacking food, water and shelter, prompted international action.

UN Security Council Resolution 688

On 5 April the Security Council adopted resolution 688 (1991) on the Iraqi refugee crisis, by 10 votes to 3 (Cuba, Yemen and Zimbabwe) with 2 abstentions (The People's Republic of China and India).

The non-mandatory resolution demanded an end to the repression of the Iraqi civilian population, 'including most recently in Kurdish populated areas, the consequences of which threaten international peace and security in the region'. It insisted that the Iraqi authorities allow immediate access for international humanitarian organisations to provide relief aid in all parts of Iraq. The resolution also appealed to UN member states to contribute to humanitarian relief efforts.

British Attitude

Sir David Hannay said that the resolution sent a clear message to the Iraqi regime that it must stop 'the repression, the harrying and

A British officer giving a press briefing in the Saudi capital, Riyadh, on the course of the allied campaign against Iraq.

Soldiers of the 3rd Battalion The Royal Regiment of Fusiliers attending a ceremony to honour their dead.

A petrol, oil and lubricant dump at Area Ray logistic base in northern Saudi Arabia.

Medical facilities at the Territorial Army's General Hospital in Riyadh.

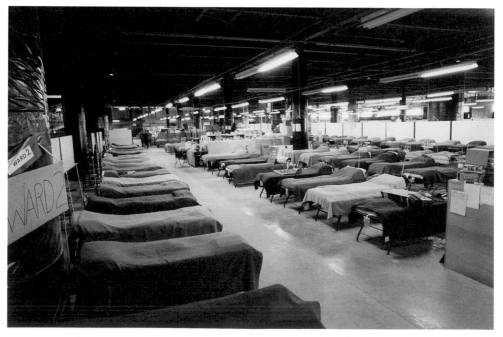

A British anti-tank launcher under camouflage netting.

Soldiers of 4th Armoured Brigade giving food and water to Iraqi prisoners of war during the ground offensive.

British soldiers practising the protective drill against nuclear, biological and chemical attack.

Blazing Kuwaiti oil wells set alight by Iraqi forces.

killing of innocent men, women and children, which is at the root of this massive exodus to Turkey and Iran'. It also gave backing to the relief efforts of UN, governmental and non-governmental organisations.

Britain, said Sir David, rejected the argument that the issue of the Kurdish refugees was entirely an internal Iraqi matter. Security Council action was justified on the grounds that:

—human rights violations were not essentially a domestic issue (which would preclude UN intervention under its Charter);

—the surge of Kurdish refugees was destabilising the whole region, threatening international peace and security; and

—Iraq had international obligations under the 1949 Fourth Geneva Convention to protect innocent civilians from violence in the case of internal armed conflicts.

Sir David emphasised that the responsibility for 'this human tragedy' lay squarely with the Government of Iraq. Its 'brutality towards its own population is only matched by its aggressive action towards its neighbours and by its disregard for international law and for all civilised standards and behaviour'.

Britain's Plan for Kurdish Refugee Protection

In the course of a meeting of the European Council in Luxembourg on 8 April 1991, Mr Major put forward an action plan designed to build on Security Council resolutions 687 and 688. The plan, which was endorsed by the Council, envisaged principally the establishment of a safe haven in northern Iraq under UN control where Kurdish refugees would be safe from attack by the Iraqi army and able to receive relief supplies.

At the same time Mr Major proposed the establishment of a register of arms sales at the United Nations to monitor and control the scale of arms build-up in any one country. He believed that this would provide 'an early warning of a country that was building up an offensive rather than a defensive capacity' and the international community would then be better placed to deal with the threat.

Operation HAVEN

In a parliamentary statement on 15 April, Mr Hurd said that the priorities of Britain's response to the Kurdish crisis were to keep the refugees alive and to create conditions in which they could return home in safety. The aim of Britain's proposal for safe havens in Iraq, he explained, was 'to create places and conditions in which the refugees can feel secure. We are not talking of a territorial enclave, a separate Kurdistan or a permanent UN presence. We support the territorial integrity of Iraq'.

On 16 April the US President announced that British, French and US forces would be deployed in northern Iraq to protect camps being set up for the Kurds. Confirming this decision, Mr Hurd said that the British Government regarded the five or six camps envisaged under the plan as temporary. He added that there were no plans to establish safe havens on Iraq's border with Iran.

The British deployment, known as Operation HAVEN, at its peak involved some 5,000 personnel (including 400 Dutch marines). These forces took part in relief operations in the mountains on the Iraq–Turkey border, including helping displaced Kurdish refugees make their way to the camps, and they provided a secure environment within which international relief organisations could operate. On 7 June relief operations were handed over to the UN High Commissioner for Refugees.

Coalition Redeployment

On 12 July the Foreign and Commonwealth Office issued a statement explaining that the aims of the relief operation undertaken by Britain and its coalition partners had been achieved. The statement noted that almost all of the 400,000 refugees who fled to the mountains in the area of the allied safe havens had returned home. British forces had helped to restore water and power supplies, to establish food distribution and basic sanitation systems, and to provide health care for those in need.

The statement declared that warnings had been issued to the Iraqi Government by the coalition members that renewed repression of the civilian population in either northern or southern Iraq would not be tolerated. No Iraqi aircraft were to fly north of the 36th Parallel, and Iraqi ground forces had to remain outside the security zone in northern Iraq set up by coalition forces.

Concluding, the statement said: 'The forces which remain in the region will continue to act as a deterrent to any Iraqi behaviour which might threaten peace and security. They will be prepared, if circumstances so demand, to respond swiftly: to go back in, if necessary, to protect the safety of the refugees and UN personnel and to take any other action as may be required.'

With an effective UN presence in place in northern Iraq, British, French and US troops were redeployed in mid-July, leaving a residual deterrent force based in southern Turkey. With the co-operation of the Turkish Government, this force has since maintained reconnaissance and other air operations above the 36th Parallel as needed in support of UN Security Council resolution 688.

Despite periodic offensive posturing by the Iraqi regime, countered by coalition warnings, the Kurds have sought to exercise a degree of autonomy within Iraq. Elections to a Kurdish assembly were held in May 1992.

Southern Iraq

In August 1992, in response to accumulating evidence of systematic government repression of the civilian population in the southern marsh area of Iraq, Britain, the United States and France agreed to establish a 'no-fly zone' for Iraqi aircraft over the area south of the 32nd Parallel.

The area is a maze of lakes and waterways supporting a population of approximately 150,000. Since the end of the uprising in March 1991 the Iraqi army has controlled the main roads into the marshes and has intensified a campaign started in 1988–89 to force the civilian population out of the area.

Iraqi military attacks against the marsh areas escalated from the beginning of 1992, inflicting substantial civilian casualties. The attacks included the use of armed helicopters, heavy artillery, tanks and, from May, fixed-wing aircraft.

In a report in mid-1992 on the situation in southern Iraq, the Special Rapporteur of the United Nations Commission for Human Rights for Iraq emphasised the need for urgent action to halt the serious violations of human rights and for effective monitoring arrangements to ensure the Iraqi Government's compliance. He also described a major Iraqi irrigation scheme which would have the effect of draining the marshlands and depriving the indigenous population of their traditional way of life as 'perhaps the greatest threat to the inhabitants of the southern marshes'.

British Position

On 18 August the Prime Minister announced that Britain would join the United States and France in monitoring the situation in southern Iraq in support of UN Security Council resolution 688.

Mr Major said that Iraqi government repression in southern Iraq was not acceptable and had to stop. 'What we propose to do is to monitor the whole area from the air, and . . . we will instruct the Iraqis not to fly in that area.' He added: 'In northern Iraq we established safe havens in order to protect the Kurds from Saddam Hussein; now it is the Shias who need protection and the international coalition have decided that that is necessary.'

In an interview on 20 August the Foreign and Commonwealth Secretary emphasised that there was no intention to dismember Iraq: 'We believe in the integrity of Iraq. Iraq is one country but, within that country, its rulers have obligations towards their subjects, which is laid down in Security Council resolution 688.'

Military Deployment

The deployment of six Royal Air Force Tornados to the Gulf region was announced by the Defence Secretary, Malcolm Rifkind, on 26 August. The purpose of the deployment was to monitor Iraq's compliance with Security Council resolution 688. Coalition aircraft would primarily have a reconnaissance role, but would also deal with any Iraqi aircraft which violated the no-fly zone.

On 27 August Mr Rifkind said: 'The Iraqi Government has been told that there must be no Iraqi aircraft in the area. . . . We hope, as with the Kurdish zone in the north, that this will also lead to a cessation of any fighting and aggression on the ground.'

United States Statement

Commenting on 26 August on the allied operation, the US President said: 'The United States continues to support Iraq's territorial unity and bears no ill will towards its people. We continue to look forward to working with a new leadership in Baghdad, one that does not brutally suppress its own people and violate the basic norms of humanity. Until that day, no one should doubt our readiness to respond decisively to Iraq's failure to respect the no-fly zone.'

Iraqi Weapons of Mass Destruction

UN Security Council resolution 687 (1991) set up a Special Commission (UNSCOM) which, with the IAEA, is overseeing the implementation of the provisions relating to the eradication of Iraq's weapons of mass destruction (see p. 35). Members of the Special Commission have been drawn from 21 countries, including Britain, and have been selected on the basis of professional expertise.

The Special Commission was mandated to carry out immediate on-site inspections of Iraq's chemical and biological weapon and missile capabilities, and to assist the IAEA in carrying out similar inspections of Iraq's nuclear capabilities, based on Iraq's declarations and any additional sites designated by the Special Commission itself.

The Special Commission is responsible for the destruction of chemical and biological weapon items and for supervising the destruction by Iraq of its ballistic missile capabilities. The IAEA is responsible for the removal of all nuclear-weapons-usable materials and for the destruction of Iraq's nuclear weapons capability. The authority of the Special Commission and the IAEA to carry out these tasks was confirmed by the UN Security Council on 17 June 1991 with the adoption of resolution 699. In addition, Iraq was required to bear the full costs involved.

Plans developed by the Special Commission and the IAEA to ensure the continued monitoring and verification of Iraq's compliance with the provisions of resolution 687 were approved by the Security Council, through the unanimous adoption of resolution 715, on 11 October 1991.

Progress of Elimination of Weapons

The Special Commission and the IAEA have undertaken a major programme of inspections since May 1991. These have produced, in spite of Iraqi obstruction and deception, important findings about the scale and sophistication of Iraq's weapons programmes.

Britain has provided specialised defensive chemical and biological warfare equipment and experts for inspections. In 1991–92, £1 million was set aside to pay for British support to the Special Commission and IAEA operations. A further £1 million was made available in 1992–93.

Iraq has consistently failed to comply fully with the obligations placed upon it by UN Security Council resolutions 687 and 707.[6] In making its original declaration, Iraq denied having nuclear or biological weapons programmes, and made no mention of a 'supergun' project. It also declared only 11,000 chemical munitions and 52 ballistic missiles.

By the summer of 1992, revised declarations and subsequent inspections had revealed:

—an extensive covert nuclear weapons development programme, in breach of the Non-Proliferation Treaty;

—a biological research programme for military purposes;

—chemical and ballistic missile development programmes;

—150,000 chemical munitions, half of which were filled, and tonnes of chemical agent and precursors; and

[6]Resolution 707, approved unanimously on 15 August 1991, demanded that Iraq provide full, final and complete disclosure, as required by resolution 687, of all aspects of its programmes to develop weapons of mass destruction and ballistic missiles with a range of over 150 km (93 miles). It further demanded that Iraq allow UN inspectors immediate access to any areas and facilities which they wished to see.

—supergun assemblies and parts.

Under the provisions of resolution 687, sanctions against Iraq will be lifted only when all Iraq's weapons of mass destruction are eliminated.

The British Government has disclosed that, by early September 1992, the following Iraqi weaponry had been destroyed under UN supervision:

—62 ballistic missiles;

—10 missile launchers;

—18 fixed Scud missile launch pads;

—32 ballistic missile warheads;

—127 missile-storage support vehicles;

—rocket fuel;

—an assembled 350 mm supergun and propellant;

—components for 350 mm and 1,000 mm superguns;

—54 items of ballistic missile production equipment;

—10 buildings related to ballistic missile production;

—11,800 unfilled chemical munitions;

—463 unstable 122 mm rockets, some filled with chemical agent;

—production equipment used in the chemical weapons pro-
    gramme;

—equipment connected to the nuclear weapons development pro-
    gramme; and

—buildings and equipment used in other areas of the nuclear pro-
    gramme (located at three separate sites).

Preparatory work for large-scale destruction of chemical weapons and bulk agent stocks began in June 1992. Two specially built destruction plants became operational at the end of 1992. The IAEA is supervising the removal of irradiated fuel.

Iraq claims to have covertly destroyed additional weapons since inspections began. None of these was included in the original Iraqi declarations. Their secret, unsupervised destruction was in breach of the requirements of Security Council resolution 687. The weapons included:

—89 ballistic missiles;

—24,470 chemical munitions;

—200 tonnes and 3,000 litres of chemical precursors;

—'various quantities' of imported and locally made parts for Scud missiles;

—25 ancillary vehicles for the Scud missile system;

—5 decoy launchers; and

—4 test and launch vehicles.

The final stage to the process is the establishment of comprehensive monitoring arrangements, in order to ensure that Iraq is not able to re-establish its weapons programmes. The commencement of such arrangements has been delayed by Iraq's failure to accept the terms of resolution 715, and by the continuing lack of a genuinely complete and final declaration of its weapons programmes, as demanded by resolution 707.

Other Issues

Compensation and Sanctions

On 20 May 1991 the UN Security Council adopted resolution 692 (1991) approving the arrangements for the establishment of a compensation fund, financed by Iraq's future oil revenues, to pay foreign governments, nationals and corporations for loss and damage caused by Iraq as a result of its invasion of Kuwait. Iraq's request for a five-year moratorium on the payment of compensation was rejected.

By a further resolution, 705 (1991) adopted on 15 August, the Security Council decided that compensation to be paid by Iraq should not exceed 30 per cent of the annual value of its oil exports.

The sanctions regime against Iraq, which has been reviewed every 60 days under the terms of Security Council resolution 687 (see p. 39), remains in force.

Two further resolutions, 706 and 712 which were adopted by the Council in August and September 1991, provided for the sale of $1,600 million-worth of oil and oil products originating in Iraq in order to meet the essential humanitarian needs of the civilian population. Iraq, however, has continued to refuse to export oil to finance humanitarian supplies and to meet claims for compensation under the terms of these resolutions.

Border Demarcation

In 1992 a United Nations Boundary Commission, set up under the terms of Security Council resolution 687, reported on its decisions regarding the demarcation of the Iraq–Kuwait land border. Kuwait will take over some more oil installations in the Rumaila oilfield and Iraqi naval facilities at the port of Umm Qasr. The rest of the port will remain in Iraqi hands. The report was endorsed by the UN Security Council on 2 October 1992.

Demarcation of the eastern section of the border, which includes the offshore boundary, is still under consideration by the Commission.

Environmental Impact of the War

The environmental havoc wrought by Iraqi forces during the war will have serious long-term consequences, given the scale of the regional pollution from oil spillage and terrestrial damage from fired and leaking oil wells.

Saddam Hussein's order to sabotage Kuwait's oil industry as his troops withdrew left more than 600 oil wells burning or gushing in the desert at the end of February 1991, contaminating the atmosphere and the land. Large quantities of oil lying in lakes around the oilfields also masked landmines and unexploded ordnance. Fire-fighting operations continued throughout much of 1991, the last oil well fire being extinguished on 6 November. The cost of putting out the fires has been estimated at $1,500 million.

Just how much oil was released into the waters of the Gulf is not known, although it is thought to have amounted to around 300,000 tonnes. The damaging effects on the Gulf's fragile ecosystem have been most evident along the Kuwaiti and Saudi Arabian coasts. International efforts to tackle the pollution continue, Britain having contributed both expert advice and specialist equipment.

Government Statements and Parliamentary Speeches

1: Speech by the then Prime Minister, Margaret Thatcher, opening the two-day debate on the Gulf crisis in the House of Commons on 6 September 1990

. . . In the early hours of 2 August, Iraq invaded and occupied Kuwait, a peaceful, independent country and a member of the United Nations since 1963. It was a flagrant and blatant case of aggression. . . .

The Government have responded to this extremely serious situation vigorously and in close co-operation with our allies and friends. Our resolute response has received wide support in this country and elsewhere, and the gratitude and appreciation of many Arab Governments. . . .

Iraq's actions raise very important issues of principle as well as of law. There can be no conceivable justification for one country to march in and seize another, simply because it covets its neighbour's wealth and resources. If Iraq's aggression were allowed to succeed, no small state could ever feel safe again. At the very time when at last we can see the prospect of a world governed by the rule of law, a world in which the United Nations and the Security Council can play the role envisaged for them when they were founded, Iraq's actions go back to the law of the jungle.

The issue is one of importance to the whole world. It affects world security, world oil supplies and world economic stability. It affects the confidence of all small states, not only those in the Middle East. We have bitter memories of the consequences of failing to challenge annexation of small states in the 1930s. We have learned the lesson that the time to stop the aggressor is at once.

The international response has been swift and resolute and for that we owe much to the United States and to the co-operation of the Soviet Union.

On 2 August, the very day of the invasion, the Security Council adopted resolution 660 condemning the invasion and calling for Iraq's immediate and unconditional withdrawal.

On 4 August, the European Community and its member states took measures to protect Kuwaiti assets, to freeze Iraqi assets, to embargo oil and to stop arms sales to Iraq. It also agreed to work for comprehensive economic sanctions in the Security Council.

Two days later, as Iraq had failed to comply with the original resolution 660, the Security Council adopted a further resolution—661— which demanded the restoration of the legitimate Government of Kuwait and imposed comprehensive mandatory sanctions on Iraq. . . . A committee of the Security Council was also set up to monitor and report on the implementation of sanctions.

Subsequently, the Security Council has adopted three further resolutions. They declare Iraq's annexation of Kuwait null and void; condemn Iraq's actions against foreign nationals in Kuwait and Iraq, and demand that they be allowed to leave; and resolution 665 calls upon United Nations member states to take necessary measures against shipping to ensure the strict implementation of sanctions. As was pointed out at the time, that includes the use of minimum force.

Not a single country voted against any of those resolutions, although the Yemen and Cuba abstained on some of them.

Let me stress: our objectives are those set out in those resolutions— unconditional Iraqi withdrawal from Kuwait and restoration of the legitimate Kuwaiti Government. The preferred method is comprehensive economic sanctions, collectively and effectively implemented.

Iraq is vulnerable to sanctions. Its economy is based almost totally on the export of a single commodity, oil, through a limited number of identifiable outlets. That is why the action of Turkey and Saudi Arabia in preventing the export of Iraqi oil through the pipelines was of such critical importance. Other outlets are being effectively blockaded, and the embargo on the sale of oil from Iraq and Kuwait is so far working well.

Iraq is also heavily dependent on imports of food and other commodities; and it has limited currency reserves following the war with Iran. That is why it was so important to freeze Kuwaiti accounts and assets abroad on the very first day, and so prevent Iraq from exploiting them. Rigorous implementation of sanctions by the whole world is vital to make the policy work. . . .

I have been dealing with sanctions and their enforcement. The question has arisen whether further authority would need to be obtained from the Security Council for military action beyond that required to enforce sanctions.

We have acted throughout in accordance with international law, and we shall continue to do so. Resolution 661, which called for comprehensive economic sanctions, expressly affirms the inherent right of individual or collective self-defence, in response to the armed attack by Iraq against Kuwait, in accordance with Article 51 of the United Nations Charter [see p. 19]. We hope that economic sanctions will prove to be sufficient. That is why they must be strictly enforced. But we are not precluded by reason of any of the Security Council resolutions from exercising the inherent right of collective self-defence in accordance with the rules of international law. . . .

To undertake now to use no military force without the further authority of the Security Council would be to deprive ourselves of a right in international law expressly affirmed by Security Council reso-lution 661; it would be to do injustice to the people of Kuwait, who are unable to use effective force themselves; it would be to hand an advan-tage to Saddam Hussein; and it could put our own forces in greater peril. For these reasons, I am not prepared to limit our legitimate free-dom of action. . . .

Our first objective has been to make sanctions effective as a means of bringing pressure on Saddam Hussein to withdraw from Kuwait. Our second but no less urgent objective was to deter further Iraqi aggression. Saddam Hussein could have gone on to invade the north-eastern terri-tories of Saudi Arabia and seize its oilfields. Had he succeeded in that, he could have taken the smaller Gulf states too. It is thanks to rapid action by the United States in sending forces to the area, and prompt support by Britain and France, that the aggressor has been halted.

We have worked throughout in the closest possible co-operation with the United States . . . at every diplomatic and military level. The President of the United States has given a lead that deserves the widest support; and the commitment of American forces has been on a tremen-dous scale.

The House will be familiar with Britain's response, which of course is on a much smaller scale—and I will summarise it briefly. We have deployed a squadron of Tornado F3 air-defence aircraft, a squadron of Tornado ground-attack aircraft, and a squadron of Jaguar aircraft for ground support. They are stationed in Saudi Arabia, Bahrain and Oman. They are backed up by VC10 tanker aircraft and Nimrod maritime patrol aircraft.

One Royal Navy destroyer and two frigates are in the Gulf. A sec-ond destroyer is on its way, as are three mine-clearance vessels. There are also a number of support ships in attendance. A limited number of ground forces are deployed to defend airfields and to provide security generally.

That is already a valuable contribution to the defence of Saudi Arabia and the Gulf, but we believe some additional forces will be needed, and their composition is under consideration.

I wish to stress three points about our armed forces. First, they have been deployed in the area at the request of the Governments of Saudi Arabia, Kuwait and other Gulf states—and, in the case of Bahrain, that Government has invoked our treaty of friendship.

Second, they arrived quickly—a factor that contributed enormously to their effect, because the greatest need to deter was in the very early days of the crisis. That is a tribute to the efficiency, skill, and dedication of our service men and service women.

Third, our forces are part of a much wider international effort, including not only United States forces but those of our European allies, of many Arab countries and others, including members of the Commonwealth. It is a truly multinational force. . . .

Our resolve, and that of our partners and allies, to bring about Iraq's withdrawal from Kuwait and the restoration of the legitimate Government is absolute. There can be no compromise solutions which limit or diminish that objective, and attempts to devise them only postpone the moment when Iraq realises that there is no option but to withdraw. . . .

In the coming weeks we must persist in the determination that we have shown hitherto. There will be those who say that the international effort is costing too much and is not worth it. Some people will forget the awfulness of what Saddam Hussein has done. There will be calls for compromise, attempts to fudge the issues and blur the principles, attempts to undermine the virtually unanimous opposition of the world to what Iraq has done. Of course we prefer a peaceful solution, but that must involve Iraq's total and unconditional withdrawal from Kuwait and the restoration of the lawful Government.

Let us not forget that in Saddam Hussein we are dealing with a person who, without warning, has gone into the territory of another state with tanks, guns and aircraft; has fought and taken that state against international law and against the will of its people. A person who will take such action against one state will take it against another if he is not stopped and his invasion reversed.

We are dealing with a person who has rejected the efforts of the Secretary-General of the United Nations to achieve a peaceful solution on the basis of the United Nations resolutions.

We are dealing with a person who plunged his country into eight years of war against Iran, costing the lives of countless thousands of Iraq's young men—and many hundreds of thousands more casualties— without achieving anything other than destruction and desolation.

We are dealing with a man who has used chemical weapons even against his own people. Such a man must be stopped; and we shall persevere until he is.

2: Parliamentary response by the then Leader of the official Opposition, Neil Kinnock, on 6 September

. . . The main focus of the debate must be on the most effective ways of depriving the Iraqi dictator and his regime of any military, economic, political or other form of gain from their aggression and of preventing him from posing any future threat to the stability and security of the region.

. . . We consider that in the circumstances arising from the invasion of Kuwait the action taken in the United Nations and in the commitment of forces was right. In the very nature of Saddam Hussein's

aggression, slowness or modesty of response would have been an invitation to him to continue over other borders and into greater excesses.

. . . It is clear that, in response to Saddam Hussein's aggression, the British people—like the world community in general—share the overwhelming conviction that intense pressure must be rigorously sustained against Saddam Hussein and his regime. Iraq's isolation must be complete. That course is supported not only as a way of avoiding or reducing bloodshed but as the best means of securing an acceptable and enduring outcome to the crisis. The widespread and, in our view, entirely correct approach is that sanctions should be given the fullest possible opportunity of working in order to make Saddam Hussein completely fulfil the requirements of the United Nations resolutions. . . .

With regard to the legalities, it is clear that military action under Article 51 is lawful if the now exiled but 'legitimate' Government of Kuwait calls for it. Such action is lawful if Saddam Hussein launches further military aggression against any state or armed forces. It is lawful if, at some time, the United Nations judges that the action taken thus far has been 'inadequate' for the purpose of fulfilling its resolutions, in which case military action under Article 42 of the Charter could be taken. . . . But we have to recognise the current reality that the potential consequences of taking action that does not have complete and unarguable United Nations' authority include further turmoil, terrorism, an increase in nationalism and fundamentalism, and possibly the destabilising of strategic allies. These are the reasons why it is important strategically . . . that everything possible is done to ensure that if further military action is necessary it should be taken under the full authority of the United Nations.

It is essential . . . that after the primary objectives of the United Nations resolutions have been attained, there must be, first, a complete and sustained embargo imposed both on arms sales and on the provision of arms manufacturing equipment to Iraq. Secondly, Iraq's chemical weapons and its chemical weapon-manufacturing capacity must be destroyed. Thirdly, provision must be made for the thorough and continual monitoring of the nuclear plant and weapons-making capability of Iraq. Fourthly . . . Iraq must make reparations, especially to the poor countries that have been further impoverished by its aggression. . . .

Saddam Hussein may well retain his position in his country in the wake of this crisis; however, he cannot be allowed to retain his power to jeopardise the region. The crisis has been inflicted upon the world by the ambition and aggression of Saddam Hussein. No one will be unaffected by the economic effects of what the Iraqi dictator has done. Millions of people in his country and elsewhere are experiencing and will experience great misery because of his actions. Some, including refugee children, have already died and thousands have lost their liberty. The world must now impose its will upon Saddam Hussein. His defeat must be a victory for the international community.

3: Announcement on 14 September by the then Secretary of State for Defence, Tom King, of the Government's decision to send an armoured brigade to Saudi Arabia

The Government has today decided to send the 7th Armoured Brigade to Saudi Arabia. This substantial army formation will represent a most significant addition to the multinational efforts in support of the Kingdom of Saudi Arabia and the other threatened Gulf states to prevent further aggression from Iraq and to reinforce the United Nations' embargo.

This armoured brigade will comprise in excess of 6,000 troops. It will consist of two armoured regiments with some 120 Challenger tanks, an armoured infantry battalion equipped with Warrior armoured fight-

*ing vehicles, an armoured recce squadron equipped with Scimitar com-
bat vehicles, a field regiment RA with 155-mm self-propelled guns, an
air defence battery with Javelin missiles and a full range of supporting
services, including Lynx and Gazelle helicopters.*

*In addition, the Government is reinforcing the RAF units already
in the Gulf. We are sending a further squadron of Tornado GR1 and
additional Tornado air defence aircraft.*

*Our purpose in sending further forces is twofold: first to ensure that
no further aggression can possibly succeed and that the defensive shield is
sure for Saudi Arabia and the other threatened Gulf states. Secondly, to
ensure that Saddam Hussein understands that while we seek the implementation of the United Nations resolutions by peaceful means, other
options remain available and that, one way or another, he will lose.*

*Iraq's evil aggression must be reversed, and my announcement
today confirms our determination to play our full part in the worldwide
effort to achieve this.*

4: Parliamentary statement on 22 November by Mr King on further deployments of British forces to the Gulf

*. . . I should like to make a statement on further deployments of British
forces to the Gulf.*

*It is now three and a half months since Iraq invaded Kuwait and
it has continued to defy the United Nations' demand to withdraw.
Sanctions have left Iraq increasingly isolated; the Royal Navy has
played an important part in this embargo. But Saddam Hussein shows
no sign yet of complying with United Nations resolutions, and ending
his barbaric treatment of the Kuwaiti people and the hostages whom he
has detained illegally. Moreover, there are now more than 400,000
Iraqi troops in and near Kuwait.*

It remains the Government's firm objective to resolve this crisis as soon as possible and by peaceful means. To do this, it is essential to establish a credible offensive military option. Saddam Hussein must be made to realise that he is faced with a military force which will otherwise compel him to withdraw.

The House will be aware that there are now 30 countries involved in this multinational effort by land, sea and air, and of the significant increases in forces now in Saudi Arabia and neighbouring countries. In particular, President Bush has announced very substantial increases in United States forces.

The Government believe that it is right to make a further significant contribution to this multinational effort. . . . The Government have today decided to deploy an extra brigade, a divisional HQ and supporting arms. They will join 7th Armoured Brigade in Saudi Arabia to form the 1st Armoured Division.

The additional brigade will be the 4th Brigade from Germany, with an armoured regiment of Challenger tanks, two armoured infantry battalions equipped with Warrior fighting vehicles, an armoured reconnaissance squadron, a field regiment Royal Artillery, together with engineers and other supporting services.

Additional equipment deploying with the Division will include M109 and M110 self-propelled guns, tracked and towed Rapier and two multiple-launch batteries. Lynx anti-tank helicopters and additional support helicopters will be sent. In all, some 14,000 additional army personnel will be deployed, which will bring the strength of 1st Armoured Division to some 25,000, and the total number of United Kingdom forces committed to more than 30,000.

The command arrangements that we have agreed provide for United Kingdom forces to be placed under the tactical control of a United States commander for specific actions where this makes military *sense. On the same basis, 1st Armoured Division may have a United States brigade assigned to its tactical control. . . . The Government have also decided to send two more mine countermeasures vessels to the Gulf. . . .*

The formation of a United Kingdom armoured division will represent a potent increase in the fighting capability of British forces in Saudi Arabia. With the further major American deployments, and the continued build-up of units from 30 other countries in the multinational force, the deployment that I have announced today is the clearest possible message to Saddam Hussein that there is a credible military option, and that he must now observe resolution 660, end his aggression, release the hostages and leave Kuwait.

5: Review of developments by the Foreign and Commonwealth Secretary, Douglas Hurd, in his speech opening the second House of Commons debate on 11 December

. . . Today is an occasion to step back from immediate events, to look at the crisis as a whole and to consider what is at stake. One immediate event is wholly welcome, and that is the release of hostages which is now under way [see p. 10]. *The total British community in Iraq and Kuwait was just over 1,100 at the time of President Saddam Hussein's last announcement. Aircraft have been chartered from Iraqi Airways to bring our people home and we have taken space on charters organised by others. . . .*

President Saddam Hussein is now complying with one of the three main requirements of the Security Council. Attention can now focus on the other two requirements—the unconditional withdrawal of Iraqi forces from Kuwait and the restoration of the legitimate government. Ten days ago I was in New York to join in the last Security Council debate on the subject. It was a notable and dramatic occasion. The Council adopted, with just two votes against, resolution 678, which empowers the international community to use 'all necessary means' to secure compliance with its earlier resolutions if Iraq does not leave Kuwait on or before 15 January next year. . . . The phrase 'all necessary means' includes the use of force. Resolution 678 is not a call to arms or a timetable for military action. The resolution provides for what it calls a pause of goodwill. . . . It gives Saddam Hussein a final opportunity to leave peacefully. We hope he takes it. . . .

I come now to the pressures that the international community— not just Britain and America—is exerting on Iraq. More than four months after the aggression, those pressures are all peaceful. The most important of them are sanctions . . . and the build-up of allied forces representing the so-called military option. There are signs in Iraq that sanctions are having an effect. Basic foodstuffs have been rationed since September. But the Iraqi people are used to hardship. They endured eight years of one of the most bloody and futile wars since 1945—the Iraq–Iran war. It must be questionable whether sanctions, even if applied over a long period, will undermine the resolve of Saddam Hussein to keep his grip on Kuwait.

Meanwhile . . . day by day Kuwait is being obliterated from the map. We can read what the hostages are saying as they come back, and we can read the Amnesty report and listen to the Kuwaitis. There is no secret about what is happening. Whatever can be removed has been taken to Baghdad. Murder, torture and brutality have been commonplace, as the Amnesty report [see p. 16] and later evidence shows. With each day that passes, the likelihood that we shall be able to restore Kuwait to its former position decreases. The Iraqi aim is clear. Iraq is out to eradicate Kuwait as an independent nation. We all welcome the return of foreign hostages from Iraq, as we have just done, but we should not forget the thousands of Kuwaitis who are virtually hostages and prisoners in their own city.

President Saddam Hussein's sophisticated war machine will continue to take advantage of the time allowed to improve its military position. There are now nearly 300,000 Iraqi troops and nearly 2,000 tanks in Kuwait, and work continues every day on improving the defences. Every delay risks increasing the casualties in an eventual conflict. Those are sobering facts which the House needs to take into account in assessing the situation. . . .

By 15 January the sanctions will have been in operation for five and a half months and an assessment has to be made. . . . People may say that sanctions are producing decisive shortages which may lead to Saddam Hussein changing his mind. That would produce a new situation but, as I have said, in our view that is not so.

In August Her Majesty's Government committed their forces to the Gulf region for a number of reasons. The first was to defend Saudi Arabia and the other Gulf states. The second was to deter Saddam Hussein from pursuing his military adventure further. Many other countries, including some of our closest friends and allies, have committed their forces with the same intentions. Those two objectives of defence and deterrence have already been achieved without any military action.

The third reason for sending our troops to the region was to back the United Nations demand—not that of Britain or America—that Saddam Hussein should withdraw from Kuwait. By the middle of January, Britain will have more than 30,000 troops in the area and they will stand beside more than 500,000 others, most of them from the United States and Saudi Arabia itself. . . . I am satisfied that this accumulation of allied force provides the strongest single hope for a peaceful outcome. Nevertheless . . . this country faces a risk of war, and in that situation every hon. Member is entitled to know . . . why that risk is justified. . . .

It is not a question of who should rule Iraq—that is not a matter for us. It is not a matter of the price of oil or access to oil. If that were the issue, everyone would have settled with Saddam Hussein long ago. It is not a matter of an American—let alone a British—desire to impose some permanent presence in the Gulf. As the House knows, we are there because friendly states out of their alarm and anxiety asked us to return. . . .

It has taken the world a long time to create even the beginnings of a system of collective security. . . . For the 40 years of the cold war, the Security Council worked imperfectly, and too often it was ineffective. Things have started to change, and we have begun to make the United Nations work. All five permanent Security Council members are meeting frequently, talking openly, and acting constructively together. We have the same aims. In fact, we have a better chance of collective security than at any other time this century. But there is a subscription to pay—if one may so put it—for collective security, in terms of collective action when aggression occurs. . . .

The latest Security Council resolution—resolution 678—is not a bluff. The legal authority to use force has been there for some time, and the political authority has now been given by the Security Council. . . .

The existence of the military option is the strongest possible expression of collective security, and the strongest possible incentive for Iraq to reverse its aggression. That military option is gaining formidable strength on the ground and in the air, and Britain is adding notably to that strength.

The aim is a peaceful solution. The Iraqis see the array that is now building up against them. They know of the authority that is backing that array, which now comes from so many nations, and from the United Nations. . . . They have a powerful incentive and reason to comply. Let us keep the message clear. . . . If the aggressor stays in Kuwait, he will be forced out; if he leaves Kuwait and complies fully with the Security Council resolutions, then he will not be attacked.

There is a peace option. It is in Saddam Hussein's hands. We are working for peace and will go on working for peace, but the doctrine of peace at any price leads not to safety but to danger.

6: Parliamentary response by the spokesman for the official Opposition, Gerald Kaufman, on 11 December

. . . Four months after the outbreak of the crisis, it is important to recall how it began. Many right hon. and hon. Members will wish to discuss the issue of force—whether it is right to use it and, if so, at what point and with what justification. It is understandable and right that the House should consider so grave a possibility. Further, it is right to remember that force has already been used in this crisis. Force started this crisis, with the unprovoked military invasion by Iraq of Kuwait, an innocent and peaceful neighbour. . . .

There is one simple and obvious way for the crisis to be resolved peacefully and without further bloodshed and loss of innocent lives, and that is for Iraq to reverse its act of aggression and withdraw from the territory that it holds illegally and against every principle of international law. Let Iraq withdraw now. If Saddam Hussein does not withdraw speedily, two options remain to secure his compliance with the United Nations resolutions—the use of force, and the use of sanctions. . . .

We take a very clear view . . . that, in the end, the will of the United Nations must prevail. That is the key criterion: the will of the United Nations must prevail, preferably without the use of force, but in resolution 678 the United Nations has now authorised the use of force. We hope that it will not be used, but it is there with the United Nations' authority to be used.

There are two reasons why we in the Labour party take the view that Saddam Hussein cannot be allowed to remain in Kuwait and why we say that unequivocally. First, if Iraq was allowed to retain Kuwait despite the clearly and repeatedly expressed determination of the United Nations that he should get out, he would, quite simply, have won. He would know that he had defied the international community with impunity.

An Iraq that had swallowed Kuwait and got away with it would be an Iraq that bestrode the Middle East. It would be an Iraq with the power already to wage chemical and biological warfare and with nothing to stop it from acquiring nuclear weapons. A triumphant Iraq which, having got away with one act of aggression and taken control of 20 per cent of the world's oil, might at some stage feel free to move further into Saudi Arabia and the Gulf states. It might feel free to absorb Jordan, and it might confront Israel. . . . The second reason why Iraq cannot be allowed to remain in Kuwait is that if it did so, that would shatter the United Nations. . . .

We are clear that the United Nations is being tested by this crisis. Twelve Security Council resolutions have been carried—the strongest series of resolutions ever carried by the Security Council. The resolutions authorised sanctions, blockade and force. If they are not complied with, the Security Council will have been seen to be nothing but an empty and futile talking shop. There will be no point in the Security Council passing any more resolutions on anything. There will be no point in it having any more meetings on anything. There will be no point in the Security Council even existing. Chaos will rule the world. . . .

I want to send a signal to Saddam Hussein that the Labour party is unequivocal in its support of the United Nations, that we do not pick and choose between the Articles of the Charter or between Security Council resolutions; that we accept the entire Charter; that we uphold all the resolutions; and that we shall not yield or rest in our determination that order shall rule in the world and that that order shall be based on the authority of the United Nations Organisation.

7: Prime Minister John Major's parliamentary speech on 15 January 1991 marking the expiry of the United Nations deadline for an Iraqi withdrawal from Kuwait

. . . Since the invasion on 2 August the international community has collectively and repeatedly called on Saddam Hussein to withdraw from Kuwait; twelve Security Council resolutions have been passed, either unanimously or with very substantial majorities, and dozens of visits to Baghdad and appeals to Saddam Hussein have been made by international statesmen from many countries. . . .

Despite all this, Iraq is still in Kuwait and shows no imminent signs of leaving. I fear that the contrary is the case. In recent weeks Iraq has continued to increase the size of its forces in and around Kuwait. There are now nearly 600,000 troops, more than 4,000 tanks and more than 3,000 artillery pieces. Its defences are continually being strengthened. Chemical weapons, already used by Saddam Hussein against his own people, have been deployed. Contrary to international agreements, Iraq has produced and threatened to use both chemical and biological weapons, the use of which would be wholly contrary to international agreements. Iraq also continues to develop a nuclear weapon, although we do not believe thus far that she has succeeded in doing so.

. . . Iraq has used military force to wipe Kuwait off the face of the map and to plunder its resources. Nor is that all. Intimidation, torture and murder of the Kuwaiti people has continued without respite. . . . Hundreds of thousands of Kuwaitis have been forced to leave their country as a part of a systematic effort to change populations, to expunge

records and to erase national identity itself. At the start of August, there were 700,000 Kuwaitis in Kuwait; today there are 250,000, a fall of two-thirds. . . .

What we are seeing is not just a simple dispute or everyday differ-ence of opinion. What we are witnessing in Kuwait is an attempt to eliminate an entire state by a dictator who has shown himself to be a thorough force for evil in his actions over recent years.

Despite all this, neither we nor our international partners have given up our efforts to find a peaceful solution on the basis of full imple-mentation of the United Nations resolutions. The United Nations, the European Community, the Arab League and the Organisation of the Islamic Conference have all separately tried to persuade Iraq to comply with the Security Council resolutions. Many individual countries and governments have made their contribution. And yet, what happened last week when Secretary Baker met the Iraqi Foreign Minister in Geneva to try yet again to bring about a peaceful solution [see p. 17]? Tariq Aziz refused even to mention Kuwait or to discuss withdrawal. He showed no flexibility or, shockingly, any remorse for the crimes that have been committed in Kuwait since the beginning of August. And an invitation to Tariq Aziz to meet the European Community was brusquely and immediately rejected and ignored.

Subsequently, as the House knows, the United Nations Secretary-General travelled to Baghdad to offer his good offices. We welcomed that unreservedly. Even at that late stage we hoped that reason would prevail. . . . Yet his involvement demonstrated, perhaps more clearly than anything else could, that the confrontation is not just between the United States and Iraq, or the West and Iraq, but between the United Nations and an aggressor that has overrun a neighbouring small and innocent country.

But I am sorry to report that the Secretary-General's efforts, too, were crudely and brutally brushed aside. When I spoke to him yesterday he told me, without any doubt or hesitation, that there was nothing favourable to report from his meeting with Saddam Hussein; not the slightest sign of willingness to comply with the Security Council resolution either now or in the future. . . .

In parallel with those diplomatic efforts, the international community has, with very few exceptions and contraventions, applied economic sanctions against Iraq. As the House knows, they are among the most sweeping sanctions ever agreed by the United Nations. They have interrupted 90 per cent of Iraq's foreign trade and have caused widespread dislocation of its economy.

What is the real test of the sanctions? It is not just whether they cause economic misery in Iraq. The real test is whether they bring about Iraq's withdrawal from Kuwait. So far, they have failed to achieve that. . . . It is clear that the sanctions will not succeed by the deadline set by the United Nations for Iraq's withdrawal from Kuwait, or for a very long time after that.

There are those who argue—and I understand their concern—that we should give sanctions more time to work. But at what price should we give them more time to work? Allowing more time for sanctions to work has other implications. . . . It also means more time for Iraq to continue to extinguish Kuwait. It means more time for Iraq to prepare its defences against allied troops and perhaps a greater subsequent cost in the lives of allied troops. It means more time during which Kuwaitis will be tortured or killed. Because sanctions are not having their intended effect, we would, in addition, in practice be extending the deadline for Iraq's withdrawal while relaxing pressure on Iraq to comply. . . .

To do so would destroy the credibility of the international community's response to Iraq's aggression, and that is why I do not believe that we have the time, nor would we be wise, to let sanctions run a lengthier and fuller course. That is the situation that we face. . . .

Peaceful means of persuading Iraq to withdraw . . . have been tried for six months now, but without success. A line has to be drawn somewhere, and it has been drawn—not hastily by us or by any one state, but deliberately and collectively by the United Nations Security Council with resolution 678.

From tomorrow the situation changes. We continue to hope and to look for a peaceful solution, but from tomorrow we shall also be justified in using all necessary means of bringing about Iraq's withdrawal; and that includes the use of force. . . .

The principles at stake are crucial, and we must uphold them. First . . . there is a clear dividing line between what is right and what is wrong, and what Saddam Hussein has done in Kuwait is, in the simplest and clearest terms, just plain wrong and unforgivable. . . .

Secondly, if he were to get away with his aggression and gain from it, other small countries in the vicinity, and those elsewhere in the world with large and potentially aggressive neighbours, will all too likely face similar problems and similar dangers. That is the second reason why there can be no deals, no partial withdrawal and no artificial linkage to solutions of other problems—nothing but absolute commitment to implement the Security Council's resolutions in full and without delay.

Thirdly, the failure to secure Saddam Hussein's withdrawal would have grave implications for the balance of power throughout the Middle East. It would mean putting off difficulties today at the expense of greater difficulties in the not too distant future—greater difficulties made more intransigent as Iraq acquires even more devastating and dangerous weapons and as its appetite for success and conquest grows.

But there is a fourth, overriding point. We have made progress, particularly over the past 12 months, towards establishing in many ways a more peaceful world in which there is greater respect for the United Nations and its resolutions. At last it has seemed that the United

Nations might live up to the aspirations of its founders. All our hopes for that would fall away if we were to allow Saddam Hussein to get away with swallowing up Kuwait in the way that he proposes. It simply cannot, must not and will not be permitted. So, if we are to have that safe world, we must demonstrate conclusively that aggression cannot succeed. If we fail to do so, when nearly the whole world is united against Iraq, we will face a heavy penalty ourselves for any future aggression. Much of the responsibility would rest with us.

For all those reasons, we have all made clear to Saddam Hussein that he must withdraw. We have also made it clear that, if he leaves Kuwait and returns within the borders of Iraq, force will not be used against him. Let me reiterate that point: if he voluntarily retreats and withdraws into Iraq, he will not be attacked there. But if he does not leave, force will be used and he will be expelled from Kuwait.

8: Mr Major's statement to the House on 17 January on the outbreak of hostilities in the Gulf

. . . I shall make a statement on the start of hostilities in the Gulf in the small hours of this morning.

Aircraft of the multinational force began attacks on military targets in Iraq from around midnight Greenwich Mean Time. Several hundred aircraft were involved in the action, including a substantial number of RAF aircraft. The action was taken under the authority of United Nations Security Council resolution 678 which authorises use of all necessary means, including force, after 15 January to bring about Iraq's withdrawal from Kuwait. . . .

The instructions issued to our pilots and those of other forces are to avoid causing civilian casualties so far as possible.

Our aims are clear and limited. They are those set out in the United Nations Security Council resolutions: to get Iraq out of

Kuwait—all of Kuwait; to restore the legitimate government; to re-establish peace and security in the area; and to uphold the authority of the United Nations.

... It is only with the greatest reluctance that we have come to the point of using force as authorised by the Security Council. We did so only after all peaceful means had failed and Saddam Hussein's intransigence left us no other course. We have no quarrel with the people of Iraq. We hope very much for a speedy end to hostilities. That will come about when Saddam Hussein withdraws totally and unconditionally from Kuwait. Our military action will continue until he comes to his senses and does so.

9: Speech in the Commons by Mr Kinnock on 21 January defining the Opposition's policy on the Gulf crisis

... Our forces are now engaged in fighting for the lawful purposes set out in the resolutions of the United Nations Security Council.

My party has endorsed those resolutions repeatedly. We consider the fulfilment of those resolutions to be critical to the future authority of the United Nations, and British forces—along with others in the coalition—are being used for the precise purpose of maintaining international law and sustaining the authority of the United Nations. They are doing their duty bravely and will continue to do so. It is our duty to give them our firm backing, and that we do. ...

Meanwhile, as the war rages, two points must fairly be made: first, Saddam Hussein shows absolutely no inclination to comply with the basic requirements of the United Nations and quit Kuwait. On the contrary, all his words are of fanatical defiance, and all his actions of military offence. Secondly, it must be said that, by withdrawing from Kuwait, Saddam could have prevented any possibility of war. Even now, he can stop the war immediately by withdrawing from Kuwait and laying down his arms. Whatever else may be said or thought about the Iraqi dictator, some things are obvious: he wilfully refused to follow a course that guaranteed no war; he does not as yet want peace, and he will not as yet allow peace. If he does, he will get peace. . . .

The war aims of liberating Kuwait from occupation and restoring the legitimate government are precise and limited, and rightly so. However, the peace aims must be broader. They must relate not just to the crime that Saddam Hussein committed against international law by invading Kuwait last August; they must also relate to depriving him of the ability to commit such a crime again. The war aims do not relate to the dismembering of Iraq, and rightly so. That would provoke instability, not prevent it.

Peace aims must therefore include the purpose of keeping Iraq whole and secure from outside attack after the cessation of this war. The war aims do not include the deposing of a government or the death of a dictator, and rightly so. They are not fit objectives for the United Nations. But the peace aims must involve the substantial disarming of Iraq by the reduction of conventional forces and the verified and complete removal of chemical, biological and nuclear weapons and the means of making them. . . .

That unavoidably means that, in the wake of this war, the peace aims must be geared to the stability of the whole of the Middle East. That requires firm and dependable long-term security structures for the region, as the Prime Minister indicated. It requires freedom from the fear of invasion or attack for nations. For peoples, it requires the recognition of their identity and their right to self-determination in their own homeland. Stability in the Middle East demands, in short, collective security operated through a United Nations with the influence to achieve political resolutions to disputes and the power to deter aggres-

sion. That influence and power cannot be wielded by one nation or by a group of nations—certainly not a grouping of nations—from outside the Middle East.

10: Parliamentary statement by Mr King on 25 February after the launch of the allied ground campaign

... The final phase for the liberation of Kuwait and the achievement of the United Nations resolutions was launched in the early hours of Sunday, 24 February. After more than six months of international endeavour to achieve a peaceful resolution of the crisis, the continuing refusal of Iraq to comply with the UN resolutions, and the rejection of the final deadline from the coalition, left us no alternative but to proceed with the final ground campaign. The need for this was further confirmed by the fact that, at the very time that Tariq Aziz was still purporting to negotiate in Moscow, Saddam Hussein was giving orders for the wholesale destruction of Kuwait and its oilfields, and for further outrages against its citizens.

The land operations involve forces of no fewer than 11 countries: the United States, Saudi Arabia, the United Kingdom, Egypt, France, Syria, the United Arab Emirates, Bahrain, Qatar, Oman and, of course Kuwait. They have now been under way for 38½ hours. So far, progress has been rapid and relatively little opposition has been encountered.

Excellent planning and preparation and, above all, determination have enabled the coalition forces rapidly to penetrate the extensive obstacle belt that the Iraqis had constructed both along the Saudi–Kuwait border and along a substantial part of the Saudi–Iraq border.

To the east of that front, coalition forces have now advanced well into Kuwait and have taken a significant number of prisoners. Many of the Iraqi units encountered surrendered almost immediately.

To the west, United States, United Kingdom, Saudi and French forces have mounted an operation into Iraq against Iraqi forces supporting the occupation of Kuwait. Some elements are encircling Iraqi units; others are breaking through defensive positions and beginning to engage Iraqi units directly. The 1st British Armoured Division is fully involved in the thrust and is now moving steadily forward.

The Saudis have announced that the number of prisoners of war taken by the coalition has now risen to 20,000. Casualties on the coalition side have been very light. . . . On my latest information, there have been no British casualties in the main advance.

In support of the land advances, allied air forces, including British aircraft, have continued their attacks both on strategic targets in Iraq and on the Iraqi ground forces in Kuwait and Iraq. The attacks are continuing in spite of poor weather conditions and without serious interference from the smoke of burning oil wells.

Maritime and amphibious forces in the northern Gulf are playing their part in the coalition attack. In particular, the Royal Navy is playing a crucial role in mine clearance operations.

11: Announcement by the Prime Minister Mr Major to the House on 28 February 1991 of the suspension of offensive military operations in the Gulf

. . . In the early hours of this morning, after consulting us and other coalition partners, President Bush announced our decision to suspend offensive military operations in the Gulf, with effect from 5 o'clock GMT this morning. We took that decision as soon as it became clear that Kuwait had been liberated and that Iraq's army had been comprehensively defeated. We took the view immediately that there could be no question of continuing to attack an army that had been defeated,

notwithstanding the lack of a surrender by its commanders. By that time, 42 Iraqi divisions had been effectively destroyed. At the latest count, coalition forces have captured, destroyed or disabled more than 3,700 Iraqi tanks, out of 4,200 in the theatre; more than 2,100 artillery pieces, out of 3,100 in the theatre; and more than 1,800 armoured vehicles, out of 2,800 in the theatre. There are 60,000 Iraqi prisoners documented so far, with many thousands more yet to be recorded.

Remaining Iraqi personnel should withdraw from the theatre of operations but should leave behind their equipment and weapons. Should Iraq resume attacks on coalition forces, or Scud attacks on any country, we shall be free to resume military operations. Meanwhile, we shall take whatever steps are necessary to defend the security and safety of our own forces. We also require the Iraqi Government to nominate military commanders to meet our own commanders within 48 hours to discuss the military aspects of a ceasefire, including the immediate release of prisoners of war.

There will be separate discussions on the political aspects. The United Nations Security Council will be asked to meet soon to discuss the necessary political arrangements for the war to end. We have spelt out the conditions that Iraq must meet for there to be a formal and permanent ceasefire. Iraq must immediately release British and other prisoners of war, as well as all Kuwaiti detainees, and return the remains of those who have lost their lives. We are already in touch with the president of the International Committee of the Red Cross to urge that organisation to redouble its efforts to secure immediate access to allied prisoners.

We shall insist on the fullest co-operation from the Iraqi military authorities to locate land- and sea-mines, explosives and other booby traps in and around Kuwait. We shall also insist on a public and authoritative statement from the highest levels of Iraq's leadership of its intention to comply fully with all the relevant Security Council resolutions. This must include renunciation of Iraq's claim to Kuwait and acceptance of Iraq's responsibility to pay reparations for the damage that its aggression has caused.

The economic and commercial sanctions being applied against Iraq will remain in force until Iraq has accepted all the Security Council resolutions and the Security Council itself has decided that sanctions should be lifted. Through the United Nations, we shall also seek a commitment from Iraq to destroy, under international supervision, all its ballistic missiles and weapons of mass destruction, and not to acquire such weapons in the future.

I am sure that the whole House will join me in congratulating the forces of the United States and the other coalition forces on their historic and comprehensive victory, which has destroyed Iraq's offensive military capability. We are thankful that it has been achieved with very few coalition casualties indeed. . . .

The war has been won. Now we have to set about establishing a durable peace. . . . Such a peace . . . must provide for the security of Kuwait and of other countries in the Gulf. Also it must deal with the other problems of the region, above all that of the Palestinians. In considering our future dealings with Iraq, we should be clear that our quarrel has been with the Iraqi leadership not the Iraqi people, who are themselves victims of the war to which Saddam Hussein condemned them. I hope that in the period ahead we can maintain the remarkable unity of the international coalition, which has been so important a factor in our success so far.

Index

Printed in the UK for HMSO.
Dd 295922, 2/93, C30, 5673, 51-2423.

A MONTHLY UPDATE

ASPECTS OF BRITAIN

Current Affairs
a monthly survey

September 1992 Vol 22 No 9

London Conference on Former Yugoslavia
Outcome of the EC/UN Peace Conference

Balance of Payments 1991
Balance of Payments 'Pink Book'

Iraq
Deployment of Allied Military Aircraft over Southern Iraq

Research and Development
The Government's Annual Review of R & D

Regional Trends
Analysis of Regional Contrasts in Britain

CURRENT AFFAIRS:
A MONTHLY SURVEY

Using the latest authoritative information from official and other sources, *Current Affairs* is an invaluable digest of important developments in all areas of British affairs. Focusing on policy initiatives and other topical issues, its factual approach makes it the ideal companion for *Britain Handbook* and *Aspects of Britain*. Separate sections deal with governmental; international; economic; and social, cultural and environmental affairs. A further section provides details of recent documentary sources for these areas. There is also a twice-yearly index.

Annual subscription including index and postage £35·80 net.
Binder £4·95.

Buyers of Britain 1993: An Official Handbook *qualify for a discount of 25 per cent on a year's subscription to* Current Affairs *(see next page).*

HMSO Publications Centre
(Mail and telephone orders only)
PO Box 276
LONDON SW8 5DT
Telephone orders: 071 873 9090

THE ANNUAL PICTURE

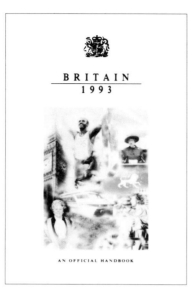

BRITAIN HANDBOOK

The annual picture of Britain is provided by *Britain: An Official Handbook* - the forty-fourth edition will be published early in 1993. It is the unrivalled reference book about Britain, packed with information and statistics on every facet of British life.

With a circulation of over 20,000 worldwide, it is essential for libraries, educational institutions, business organisations and individuals needing easy access to reliable and up-to-date information, and is supported in this role by its sister publication, *Current Affairs: A Monthly Survey.*

Approx. 500 pages; 24 pages of colour illustrations; 16 maps; diagrams and tables throughout the text; and a statistical section. Price £19·50.

Buyers of Britain 1993: An Official Handbook *have the opportunity of a year's subscription to* Current Affairs *at 25 per cent off the published price of £35·80. They will also have the option of renewing their subscription next year at the same discount. Details in each copy of* Handbook, *from HMSO Publications Centre and at HMSO bookshops (see back of title page).*

CASPIN SEA

TURKEY

SYRIA

IRAN

JORDAN

IRAQ

SAUDI ARABIA

KUWAIT

THE GULF

Mardin
Urfa
Al Hasakah
Ar Raqqah
Dayr az Zawr
Anah
Ar Rutbah
Ar Rafha
Turayf
Ar'ar
Rafha

Zakho
Amadiyah
Dahuk
Al Qamishli
Mosul
Tall Afar
Arbil
Rawandiz
Mahabad

Sulaymaniyah
Halabja
Sanandaj
Kirkuk
Tuz Khurmatu
Tikrit
Samarra
Qasr-e-Shirin
Khanaqin
Mandali
Ilam
Kermanshah
Hamadan

Hit
Ar Ramadi
Ba'qubah
BAGHDAD
Badrah

Karbala
Al Hillah
Al Kut
Nukhayb
An Najaf
Ad Diwaniyah
Ar Rifa'i
Al Amarah

As Samawah
An Nasiriyah
Ash Shabakah
As Salman
Al Busayyah

Al Basrah
Khorramshahr
Abadan
Az Zubayr
Umm Qasr

KUWAIT CITY

Zanjan
TEHRAN
Qom
Hamadan
Arak
Kashan
Khorramabad
Esfahan
Dezful
Masjed Soleyman
Ahvaz
Behbehan
Bandar Khomeyni
Bushehr

Lake Urmia
Buhayrat al Asad
Mileh Tharthar
Bahr al Milh
Euphrates
Tigris
Diyala
Great Zab
Lesser Zab
Khabur
Shatt al-Arab
Karun
Qezel Owzan
Simareh
Dez
Khersan
Zohreh
Wadi al Batin

IRAQ

—··—··— International Boundary	—⊢— Railways
—— Primary Roads	Intermittent Lakes
— — — Other Roads	✈ Int. Airport

0   100   200 Kms
0   100 Miles

38°E   40°   42°   44°   46°   48°   50°

36°N
36°
34°
34°
32°
32°
30°
30°

General Staff Map Section, GSGS 11157(CAD) Edition 2-GSGS, October 1990   299/90

Produced under the direction of Director General of Military Survey, Ministry of Defence, United Kingdom 1990